MEMOIRS OF A JERSEY FARM BOY

by PETE TUCKER

To Jim,

Hope you enjoy it.

Merry Christmas!

Pete Tucker

ACKNOWLEDGEMENT

I thank my dear niece, Krista Tucker, for prompting me to put pen to paper, or should I say fingers to keyboard, to produce these memoirs. Krista spends Christmas back here in Hunterdon County where I still say she belongs! Annually then, we convene and eventually talk about writing. Krista writes by profession. I write for giggles.

We both have an abiding faith in the virtue of leaving a permanent record. Let's face it; a few generations from now, who will even know that we had something to add to the conversation?

Write it down, dear readers, write it down!

Krista does. The Disney Co. pays her to do just that. They know talent when they read it!

Memoirs of a Jersey Farm by Pete Tucker
Published by Tuckaway Press

Cover design: A.L. Sirois
Photos courtesy of Pete and Judy Tucker
Edited by Alan Grayce
Author photograph by David W. Steele

ISBN-13: 978-1537417745   ISBN-10: 1537417746

To my partner, my pillar, my beloved wife, Judy.

FOREWORD

New Jersey gets a bad rap! What's the joke when someone says they're from New Jersey? "Oh yeah, what exit?" Surely the reply is not, "Oh yeah, where's your farm?" Truth be told, a chunk of New Jersey is a bit of a concrete jungle. A bigger bit of it is beautiful farmland. Most folks do not know that. My exit was in the depths of Hunterdon County farmland. There was, there still is, a lot of farming in progress. It's certainly where I wore out a few pairs of shoes! It was there that I was "bread and buttered" as they say.

Not that I was old enough to recall, but my older siblings tell me that I was a happy, insouciant little tyke, playing outside the summer long with nary a shirt on my back, my pants held up with a piece of baling twine. As summer waned, my hair was whitish blonde, with skin from my waist up as brown as a cola nut! Thank Heaven Mom never tried to smother me with that sunscreen goop. We never knew what it was anyway. Funny how we survived!

At some point in our lives, should we not all at least attempt to jot down some memories? How else to provide a modicum of continuity to those at our heels? To those who, sooner than you know, will be wondering just why this or that blossomed the way that it did? Believe me, the window between the generations is brief. May we not better see through it with the help of a few words? To understand the way things were will always provide one's best view into the future.

In a way, I was hobbled writing these memoirs, with both parents deceased. How soon the details about anything and everything are faded when the generations have scribed too few pertinent notes. I fear that status may worsen as I see electronic gadgets become the increasingly singular focus of young minds. Cannot someone invent the video entitled, Life on the Farm? Read on! That video may be a better play than you think!

Table of Contents

PARENTS AND GRANDPARENTS

AND IN THE BEGINNING

Mom recalled her long walk to the school bus stop as a little kid. The Capoolong Creek as well as the south branch of the Raritan River crisscrossed the family farm, a hundred-plus acres in Franklin Township. But it wasn't as though Mom's trek took her through the streams to get to the bus. It wasn't that tough a hike; it was simply the confluence of a lot of water... and a railroad that was part of the mix.

In those days, the train that passed Capoolong Farm was pulled by a steam locomotive. Each school day, Mom and her sister would amble down the lane through the locust trees, trudge over Lansdowne Road and then walk under the train trestle and up to Sidney Road, where the bus would stop.

That route had its dangers, as I remember Mom telling it. It wasn't the traffic; there was hardly any. But walking under the trestle called for a wary eye if a train happened to be passing above. Remember, that locomotive was burning coal: puffing smoke and belching hot cinders. If an ember landed on a careless school kid walking underneath, that kid got a nasty burn.

Mom told tales of the occasional arrival at Capoolong of a hobo. That's right, an honest-to-gosh hobo with all his belongings bundled in a scarf or a burlap bag, tied to a stick leaning on his shoulder. They'd jump off the train near the farm, figuring it looked prosperous enough and maybe they'd find a little work there. Mom said that her Dad saw to it that the hoboes didn't hang around too long. I guess they hopped the same train that had brought them there.

I can only imagine what it must have been like: a thoroughly rural setting. Mom, neé Janet Newton Schanze, went to school in Clinton. Her mother, Laura Jean Schanze, was, to me, everything one might wish a Grandma to be: a kind and delightful lady. About Grandpa Schanze, I only ever heard stories. He died in 1950, a few years before I was born.

In WWI, Grandpa Schanze was a gunnery officer on the *Corsair*, a re-fitted yacht that had been conscripted by the U.S. Navy from industrialist J.P. Morgan. This was one of three of Morgan's yachts to be used in that war. The *Corsair* sailed the Atlantic flanking the big ships, adding the reinforcement of extra guns, munitions and supplies. It's said of Grandpa, who was of a military bent, that he served valiantly.

A distant cousin, August Zimmer, fought for the Union in the Civil War at the second Battle of Bull Run. The Union lost that battle, but August lived to tell the tale. A faded photograph of him hangs in my house to this day. Grandpa Schanze would never have hung August's photo in the house at Capoolong. That would have been blasphemous to him. How can a soldier lose a battle and banter about it later? I can only hope that I have Grandpa's posthumous forgiveness for having Cousin August's photograph on my wall.

Grandpa was a cocky fellow. What makes me say that? Well, Grandpa's copy of the 1908 Lucky Bag, the Annapolis yearbook when he graduated. From the description of him in that yearbook, Midshipman Schanze seemed like a real over-achiever.

Truth be told, Grandpa Schanze was no farmer. He and his brother, my great-uncle Ed, tinkered with farming but they didn't produce much of anything. Grandpa was among the few who during The Depression were able to stay employed. I surmise that that's how he had the scratch to acquire Capoolong and set himself up as a gentleman farmer. There may have been some "older" money, as well.

* * *

It has been said that a woman marries a man like her father. Mom did. Clare Tucker was a lieutenant on a WWII battleship. He became a farmer, eventually, but he didn't grow up farming. That left him at a disadvantage getting started, sort of like Grandpa Schanze.

I was about two years old when the folks decided to pack it in at Capoolong. Most of my memories of it came from going back to visit after we had moved to a place in Alexandria Township, the next township over. The folks dubbed the new farm Tuckaway because it was so far from everything. Plus, of course, the obvious play on the name Tucker. Grandma Schanze remained at Capoolong.

Why didn't the folks stay where they were? Well, Grandma still owned the place and there were further tangled webs. Dad wasn't exuberant about living within the in-law's gravitational pull, although Grandpa had long since passed away. In addition, neither Mom nor Dad saw eye to eye with Aunt Laje, Mom's sister, who was still at Capoolong. Mom and Dad thought it best to get their own farm, so that's what they did.

Too bad, in a way. Capoolong was (and still is) a spectacular place. The main house is an almost palatial, pre-Revolutionary War stone Colonial with fireplaces in almost every room, and great porches. My most vivid memory is of a monstrous old bell, about the size of a mini-fridge, mounted on the front porch by Grandpa Schanze. He had gotten it from the Pennsylvania Railroad, his employer for many years. At dinnertime, that bell could easily be heard by anyone working on the farm.

I never saw it, but word was that a tunnel ran from the cellar of the house to the smokehouse, a convenient and quick escape from local Indians. Yes, in early America such dangers lurked even in New Jersey. You can bet that "intruders"— settlers—had to watch their backs, and that included the builders of the old house at Capoolong. Capoolong was surely an Indian name, not English or German.

Up the hill from the main house is another, smaller house that my Great Grandpa Gillon helped build. Prior to moving to Tuckaway we lived in this house. Great Grandpa was a stonemason in Scotland before he immigrated to America. Anyone familiar with Colonial American stonework will immediately know that this type of masonry comes from a different tradition. It is beautiful work and quite distinct from traditional early American.

I had occasion to visit a tenant in this house about 35 years ago. Any memories of the house re-kindled from my "terrible twos" were vague at best. But my siblings and I had frequent visitations back to Capoolong and Grandma Schanze. She used to whip up the best pancakes!

A sweet old lady she was, but I fear that if someone pushed the reverse button on the time machine I'd have to have a word with her. Grandma sold Capoolong Farm for $54,000.

Let's do the numbers. Two beautiful stone houses, one hundred-plus acres, a barn, plentiful water, a site rich with history in beautiful Franklin Township, Hunterdon County. $54,000! Oh, well! Who knows what a valid appraisal would have been in 1965 when she sold it? But I have to believe the buyer got a steal.

WHO NAMES THEIR SON CLARE?

Dad grew up in Michigan. Apparently, at least back then, Clare was an accepted male name around there. That is what Dad told us anyway. Curiously though, at age 62 as I write this, I've never met another guy named Clare.

There are many women named Claire, different spelling of course. There is a County Clare in Ireland (I've been there). But where is there another guy named Clare? I haven't found one!

The name constantly caused confusion for Dad. Letters in the mail were commonly addressed to Mrs. Clare Tucker. Or to Mrs. Claire Tucker. There was never really any confusion as to who the intended recipient of the letter was. Mom's first name was Janet. It wasn't as though Clare, or Claire, rhymed with Janet, and people just weren't paying attention. Occasionally, however, a telephone solicitor would ask to speak with Clare Tucker. Dad would get on the line, say hello, and the solicitor, obviously flustered, would hang up!

One time a salesman got into an argument with Dad as to whether he was really speaking with Clare. Clare became irate and hung up on him. The guy called back. Mom answered. The guy asked for Clare. Clare took the phone and said "Hello" again. The salesman hung up.

Johnny Cash once sang a tune, "A Boy Named Sue." He could have just as easily slipped Clare in there instead of Sue.

Kids eventually get a little cavalier with addressing their parents. We did. All in good fun we started calling Dad, Clare. He was OK with it. Grandma Schanze's nickname for Janet was Nan. So Mom became Nan. Clare and Nan became our standard terms of endearment.

Incidentally, Clare's middle name was Addison, in honor of a direct descendant, Joseph Addison, the English man of letters. I may have a little of Uncle Joe's DNA, but don't expect to find me in the Harvard Classics anytime soon. Of course, my niece's son, Addison, presently carries Uncle Joe's torch.

MISS MOE

Dad enjoyed telling the story about the first time he met his bride-to-be. He had just finished a Navy officer ing school; the year was probably 1941 in the Newark, w Jersey area. To celebrate the occasion, the ROTC onsored a dance attended by new officers. On one wall of the ance hall were the officers, on the other, a bevy of patriotic-minded, single ladies.

Imagine the scenario. Nobody knows anybody. The success of the whole thing depends entirely on the social capabilities of whoever is in attendance. Understandably, things were getting off to a slow start. Who goes first?

We do know this:

On one wall, weighing his options, was Clare Tucker from Mt. Morris, Michigan. On the opposite wall was Janet Schanze from Annandale, New Jersey, a student at Newark Secretarial School. For the time being, both were just sitting there.

At length, Clare gets up, walks across the dance floor and approaches Janet Schanze. He introduces himself, then comments to her on the nature of this perfectly level playing field. How was any possible coupling to be arrived at? By what means?

Clare went on to explain that, to lend fairness to the situation, he had decided which lady to ask to dance by a simple process of eenie, meanie, minie, moe!

"You, my dear lady, are Miss Moe," Clare said to Janet.

Surely, they both shared a moment of levity and proceeded to the dance floor. The proverbial ice had been broken!

I have always had two problems with Clare's story, though I never found occasion to discuss them with him. First, what does it do to a young woman's self-esteem to know that she has been asked to dance only because she is a stranger's Miss Moe? Yes, it was a clever line. No, I doubt that Clare ever considered that.

Secondly, I have seen photos of Janet that were taken close to that time. She was a pretty fine-looking filly. I also know how the male mind works. Don't tell me, Clare Tucker, that you had to do eenie meenie to figure out who you wantc for a dance partner.

Clare and Janet dated for a few months, fell in love anc decided to get married. One problem: Clare had a war to go fight in the Pacific. The battleship *Massachusetts* was Clare's home for the next two years.

THE TUCKER BROTHERS GO TO WAR

This was the big one, The Necessary War. America had been ruthlessly attacked. Pearl Harbor lay in ruins. Dad and his brother, Bud, both enlisted. There wasn't even a question in 1941; it was their duty to join the fight. If they did not, if America did not, an ugly future lay in store for the country.

I recall Dad's descriptions. His brother couldn't even talk about it fifty years after. I spoke briefly with Bud about his war experience shortly before he died. Even with that limited window provided to me by these two men, how could I not make it part of my memoirs? Their sacrifice was immeasurable.

Dad, as already noted, had met Janet Schanze. Did her father, my Grandpa Schanze, have any effect on Dad's decision to go with the Navy? No one will ever know. It was a fact, however, that the two lovebirds had already resolved to get married. Dad just had to go to war first, which was not the usual track that one's betrothal takes.

This fact alone, however, was representative of the personal sacrifices being made by Americans everywhere. Thousands and thousands of men and women took a long pause to fight the war. Some survived, many did not. All were affected one way or another.

There are thousands of stories of brothers who fought in World War II, many accounts of three or four brothers. Often a fraction came back, often none did. Both Tucker

came back. Both had their stories of a relentless
ᴄ, but, truth be told, Dad got the better end of the deal.

Dad quickly moved up through a few ranks. He sailed
the Pacific war theatre as a Lieutenant JG on the
assachusetts. The ship sailed with a huge flotilla of other
ʲattleships, destroyers, aircraft carriers and auxiliary ships, an
intimidating array. Regrettably, I never got from him many
details regarding the fighting action that he saw, but the
Massachusetts was in the thick of some notable hot spots.

My niece, Krista Tucker, some years ago taped her
interview with Dad about his war experience. For this writing, I
re-listened to the tape. Dad, suffering with Parkinson's disease,
struggled to read her the war diary he had kept. Still his stories
were compelling.

Bombardment from Japanese warplanes had been a
constant threat. The diary gave a daily accounting of what ships
were damaged, what ships were sunk by kamikazes, how many
"Jap" planes were shot out of the sky and what sailors were lost
in the "drink."

Typhoons were common. Miserable sailing and flying
conditions were standard. Dad wrote about days when damage
rendered to Japan's air forces were monumental for a day's
worth of fighting. The Japs were losing; losing badly.

Toward the end, the prospect of having to sail to the
Japanese coast loomed large. How many more years would this
war last if an attack on the Japanese mainland became reality?
Indeed, U.S. ships sailed there and commenced bombardment
of the mainland. Dad's diary recounted those events in detail.

A huge sigh of relief came with the news of a surrender
ceremony with Japanese officials that took place aboard the
USS *Missouri*. Two atomic bombs had been dropped. Dad
wrote in his diary, "What the hell was an atomic bomb?" Japan
had surrendered. It was time to sail home!

(Years ago, I knew a gentleman in Flemington named
John Krauss. John was the retired band director at Hunterdon
Central High School and a small shop owner in Flemington.
He, also, many years before, had directed the band that played
at the surrender ceremony aboard the *Missouri*. John noted

that he'd received certain orders. When the American delegation was introduced, he struck up a lively and patriotic tune. When the Japanese delegation was introduced, there was absolute stone silence. The surrender agreement was then signed.)

Sept. 15, 1945, Janet Schanze receives a most welcome telegram delivered to Capoolong:

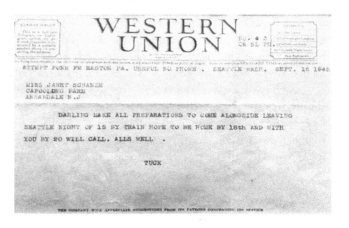

"Tuck" was coming home!

Dad's brother, my Uncle Bud, had a nightmarish war experience. At enlistment time, he wanted nothing to do with sailing on a ship. It wasn't his choice, anyway. Infantry it would be for Uncle Bud. Bud entered the war theater on D-Day. He went ashore at Omaha Beach.

The timing of the landing was behind schedule, so the tide was considerably higher than had been planned for. When the gates dropped from the amphibious landing craft, Bud saw comrades, backpacks heavily overloaded, immediately sink to their death. Bud was among the "lucky" ones, shucking his backpack so as to escape the perils of the tide and the hail of bullets, and find cover.

At length his travails found him in the Battle of the Bulge where he was taken prisoner by the "Krauts." After four months of near starvation, the POW camp where he was being held was mistakenly shelled by American artillery. The bombardment allowed Bud to escape. He was hidden by a French family for nearly two months until he was able to hook back up with another unit.

This was the unit that eventually liberated the German concentration camp at Dachau. Bud's account was harrowing; with descriptions of dead bodies stacked up like cordwood, ready for cremation.

American soldiers went into town and rousted up as many town folk as they could and marched them to this hideous camp. The locals had to see this. "Ich weis nicht," they all declared. "We didn't know." The Americans knew better.

Nearly fifty years later, a letter was received, addressed simply to: Town Hall, Mt. Morris, Michigan. USA. Its writer, Colette Berard, was one of the daughters of the French family that had hidden Bud during the war. She had no idea if the letter would ever get to him, but she implored the Mayor to try. Bud received the letter three days later. They happily corresponded for years afterward.

FAULTY LADDER

Mom's work wasn't just confined to the kitchen. She occasionally worked in the barn, too. One fateful day as she was climbing up into the haymow, the ladder broke and she fell to the concrete floor below, seriously injuring her shoulder.

Her recuperation was slow and painful. When her arm was finally out of its sling, the doctor gave her exercises to do, intended to restore mobility to her arm. She was at first totally unable to lift it. With a handsaw and wood chisel, Dad cut teeth into the side of a two by four and mounted it vertically to a wall in the house. The idea was for her to stand in front of this crude physical therapy apparatus and use her fingers to "climb" her hand up it as high as her level of pain would allow.

This was painful to watch, but not nearly as painful as it was for her. Months of this went by. Progress was slow, but eventually Mom regained full mobility to her arm. During all of this, it wasn't as though her work went by the wayside. It was just painfully slower. Mom was one stalwart woman.

MOM WAS CULTURED

Our house at Tuckaway was a little rough. Two rooms were upstairs, one larger than the other. The larger was the bedroom for brother Dave and me. Upstairs was drafty. When winter winds blew, powdery snow would find a way inside the windows. One of my favorite jokes was putting a wad of snow under Dave's covers just before he got into bed.

The other upstairs room was unfinished; that is, bare studs and no insulation. I would hang out in this room once the weather warmed up. It was a sort of getaway for a little kid. Mom had an old record player up there, I guess from her childhood. It was advanced, as far as I was concerned. One could adjust the rotation speed of the records; the single 45s, the "long playing" 33s, and the old time 78s that rotated at about 100 MPH!

Mom had a wealth of classical music on those old 78s, all neatly sheathed and stored in the cabinetry of that ancient record player. I would listen to the music of Beethoven and Brahms, Ravel and Rossini and a host of others in between.

I write these words from our accustomed winter haunt in Naples, Florida. Last evening we attended a performance of the Naples Philharmonic. They performed an eclectic program of music including the Brahms Hungarian Dance #5. I hummed along with it, and Jude expressed her surprise.

"How do you know this so well?" she inquired.

I told her about Mom's old 78s.

"I grew up with this music," I explained as I harkened back to that old unfinished room upstairs at Tuckaway.

SISTER / SISTER

Was it just a matter of old-fashioned sibling rivalry? Was it two decidedly different personalities that too often clashed? Or was it something else altogether? We shall never know, but Mom and her sister, Laje, just never saw eye to eye. (Mom, as a little girl, couldn't manage the proper pronunciation of her younger sister Laura's name. What came out was "La-jee.")

It was not uncommon for my siblings and me to hear Mom make derisive remarks about her sister, but they were trifling. Sadly, the rift persisted throughout their lives. Could it have been mended? Probably; but it was never to be. It was always my perception that Laje tried harder toward that end than Mom did, but two were in the dance.

As a kid, it was odd to me that my cousins seldom came over to play. My siblings and I seldom reciprocated. That was just the way it was, even though only a few miles separated the two families. A raw edge was there that never seemed necessary, and indeed it was not.

I suppose that this is the stuff of more than a few families, but it is instructive, nonetheless. What worth was there in any of this? Was there any validity to precedents that were set for future generations? Precedents that were surely not of their own choosing?

To what avail that Mom and her sister took these trifles to their graves?

DAD'S DIFFERENT APPROACH TO DAIRYING

Dad had to do what he had to do. Trying to get a milking herd going took time. Until there was some milk to sell, Dad worked another job with a schedule that allowed him to be home by three o'clock or so in the afternoon, in time to change clothes, take a quick nap and get to the barn. He kept that job for many years.

That, for starters, was not the way most dairy farmers in the area were doing it. Dad's different beat did not stop there. The major cost of doing business was for feed. Dairy cows consume a huge amount of feed. What was in that feed? Well, corn, oats, wheat and the like. And then there was hay, hundreds of tons of hay.

While most farmers toiled in the fields all day, growing the crops that made all of this feed, Dad bought all of his feed. Well, how was that going to work? There were no dollars in the dairying equation to allow for that.

Well, there are two sides of every equation. Dad's fellow farmers were buying seed and fertilizer. They were buying tools and tractors, equipment galore: all huge costs that Dad avoided. We had a little Ford tractor and a manure spreader. That comprised most of our equipment.

When the milk check came in the mail and all was accounted for, Dad was surely no worse off than the next farmer. Indeed, he was ridiculed for his approach, but he took it in stride. Dad thought outside the box!

CLARE, A BIT OF A RAGEAHOLIC

Yes, it's true. Clare had a temper that sometimes got the better of him. When he was reprimanding us, he would yell. When he was yelling, too often he would hit. Or whip. Our milking machines required a strap that hooked over a cow's back called a surcingle. No one wanted to get whipped with one, but it would happen.

Clare could certainly strike the fear of God into a kid. While doing my work in the barn, I would try to avoid him; sometimes hide from him. He caught me once hiding from him behind a barn door. Shame, embarrassment, fear, helplessness, they all washed over me at once. I guess Clare recognized that he had one bewildered kid on his hands. Instead of whipping, he just berated.

I suppose it is a common occurrence for kids to pledge to themselves not to do what their parents did. I frequently made that pledge as it related to Dad. In retrospect, I can surely see my Dad in myself, but I know without question that my kids did not experience what I did with my Dad. Mission accomplished, I hope.

In fairness, I can understand why Dad was the way he was. His father died when Clare was 13. His sister died in her early teens. Things in the household were grim. They were very poor; subsistence was the order of every day. Would I have been warped by such an existence? Probably.

CLARE'S LIGHTER SIDE

Despite his edge, Clare had a good sense of humor. One day he and Nan stood in line in Fall River, Massachusetts to buy tickets to tour the USS *Massachusetts*, at that time and still today a museum. Forty years earlier, Clare had hefted the bags of gunpowder that fired its 16-inch guns. These monsters required 400 pounds of powder to fire a single projectile.

The ship had sailed in the Mariana Islands, the Marshall Islands, Surigao Strait and the embattled shores of Pellileu, to name a few. Clare couldn't help but take a little umbrage at his unseemly juxtaposition: standing in line to pay to board his old battleship.

A demure little old lady sat at the ticket window, her head barely reaching visibility. As she held out her hand for money, Clare scowled. "The last time I boarded this pig iron bastard, I didn't have to pay!"

The lady just smiled and took his money. Most likely she didn't understand what he was grousing about.

FARM RAISED

OFF TO TUCKAWAY

When we moved to Tuckaway, my brother Dan was 9, sister Sue 7, Dave was 4, and I was two years old.

Where does the childhood phantasm fade away and reality take hold? As I ponder what seem to be my first conscious memories, I do wonder.

I played at my new location in a green, wood shake sided, duplex doghouse. No dogs occupied it, so it was the perfect playhouse. Noises. Distant noises conjured a variety of scenarios in my mind as I played. Our new house (not the doghouse) was half a mile from the road, so any traffic noises were muted. I suppose that that alone stirred my nascent mind to vivid imaginings.

Famed labor-law Congressman Fred A. Hartley had to divide his Alexandria Township farm about in half in order to effect a sale. Dr. Alex Mitchell and wife, Charlotte, bought part of the farm, Dad and Mom the other, thereby creating Tuckaway Farm. It was 1955. And it was a "tucked away" 62 acres.

Hartley and his wife, Hazel, had lived in what became the Mitchells' house. The place was absolutely immaculate.

They must have had a full-time gardener. It was a spacious old house with a nicely appointed circular driveway and rose bushes everywhere, giving the place an almost make-believe aura. A reservoir, a pond, a swimming pool, a fruit orchard, grape vines—the amenities were endless!

Then there was our house, a small, drab Cape Cod that had originally been a farm help house. Built during WWII when all materials were scarce, this structure was basic; it was sided with asbestos shingles, which, I soon learned, could be written on with pencil. Boy, was that fun! Boy, did I get in trouble for doing it!

The house was situated next to a detached garage, with numerous outbuildings including a large, very old barn that would become our dairy barn. Dad finally had his farm and enough work to last a lifetime—and then some!

Hartley took back a thirty-year mortgage on the farm. I think he did for the Mitchells, too. Dad's payment for principal and interest was $116 per month. Today that sounds like a piece of cake, but remember this was not in today's money. I know that Dad lay awake many a night wondering how he was ever going to make that payment. He did, though. Every month, for thirty years.

Sandy (Alexander) Mitchell was the second oldest Mitchell kid. Eventually there would be six altogether. Sandy and I were about the same age. Unless we ventured off the farm in separate directions, we were inextricably linked pals. (Much later, in teenage years, Sandy let his hair grow long. This prompted my brother Dave and I to start calling him Arlo, as in Arlo Guthrie. The nickname stuck.)

Later I'll have much more to say about the Mitchell kids and Arlo. But for now, I'll simply say thank goodness the Mitchells were cool kids. They were the only game in town. The Tucker kids didn't get off the farm much. Meanwhile, Arlo (Sandy) was the perfect tenant for the other side of the doghouse.

I'm really not sure how old I was when I first strapped on my boots to go work in the dairy barn. I'm guessing maybe six. I do remember a period when I wasn't totally up to the task, when there were lulls in my duties as I stood by awaiting further instruction. The bales of hay were probably heavier than I was, but I learned where the knife was. It didn't take much strength to cut the twine and disburse the bale, chunk by chunk, to hungry critters.

I was soon placed on Heifer Duty. That was simple enough; an easy routine to remember. Heifers were a dairy's "farm team," as in baseball. No pun intended. New, soon to lactate heifers were always needed (a minor league team, if you will) for new milking talent. Before long I was doing other work out in the barn, but heifers were my mainstay.

Lord, how my family worked! Through grade school, my brothers and I were wide-awake by 4:30 in the morning, getting booted and dressed for the barn. This wasn't just on some days, this was every day. Christmas too! Morning milking took about 2½ hours, then back at it for another two after school.

Saturdays were "hammer down" work all day, getting ready for the upcoming week. Hay needed to be moved to various barns. Cows needed clipping. Corn and barley had to be bagged for the grist truck on Tuesday. Cobwebs needed to be knocked down in prep for an impending visit from the barn inspector. Thistles needed scything in the pastures. Fence fixing was always in order. Horse stalls needed their weekly cleaning. With any luck, there would be time to ride a horse, but that rarely happened.

Decades later, in a moment of uncommon candor, Dad confessed something to me. He spoke of a nagging guilt that he'd had for many years. He had asked too much of his sons. He had worked us far too hard. I replied by observing that we really were not doing busy work, that everything we did needed to be done.

"Yeah", Dad replied. "It was the damned choice I made. Dairying was just too much work."

I remember musing to myself, Why didn't you have that moment of clarity about twenty years ago?

It has been said that there is one difference between dairy farming and being in jail; in jail, you don't have to milk cows twice a day! I guess Clare Tucker never got that memo.

Would he have paid heed to it anyway? I am inclined to guess not.

We never know the course our lives will take as a result of decisions that were made before we were born. What else to do then, but roll with the punches? Grab a pitchfork and get'r done!

NAME THAT FIELD, NAME THAT COW

Tuckaway wasn't a big farm, maybe just sixty or so acres. There were others in the neighborhood that were a hundred or even three hundred acres. This wasn't the Midwest or Manitoba, but those were big farms to us. Even so, with Dad and three boys working the farm, we often had to be specific about where we were working or else communications would gum up. To do so, we gave each field and pasture a name.

If the plan was for all to convene at two o'clock to fix fence, the next question was where? Tuckaway had a long and gangly configuration. "On the farm" wasn't good enough. It was impossible to see the 'high field' from the 'big field,' and vice versa. The 'field behind the barn' could be seen from the 'shed field' only if the leaves were off the trees. So it wasn't possible to see the 'shed field' from the 'field behind the barn' while the leaves were on the trees.

You might guess that because the big field was named the big field that it might be seen from all the other fields. No way! In fact, the big field couldn't be seen from any of the other fields. The only spot on the farm with direct visibility to the big field is where 'the three streams meet'—but the leaves have to be off the trees.

Later in life, after I bought the farm, I merged another twelve acres to it, the Baker field. Can any of the four other fields be seen from the Baker field? That depends on the leaves!

The fact was, these names helped to grease the Tuckaway machine. We didn't wander through the woods wondering how to find each other. In like manner, every cow and horse had a name.

If Dad instructed to leave Hermes in her stanchion today so the vet could come check her, we had better know which cow was Hermes, out of the thirty or so in the barn.

Yes, names surely had their place, but c'mon Dad! Hermes? He was the Greek God of Commerce, not a cow in the barn at Tuckaway! Wrong gender, anyway.

MY FIRST HAIRCUT

Jimmy Costello was a barber in Clinton for I'm not sure how many decades. He was still cutting hair when I was in my twenties, thirties and forties. He didn't start out in Clinton, though. He started in Chicago... during Prohibition.

You could about bet that Jimmy had seen it all. Remember, this was Organized Crime Chicago, Mobster Chicago, Al Capone and Elliot Ness Chicago. Later, Jimmy moved to New York City. There, one of his regular customers was Albert Anastasia, one of the most ruthless and feared Cosa Nostra mobsters in U.S. history. Turns out Anastasia and I were Jimmy's mutual acquaintances. In a different time and place; it all ended there, thankfully.

One day, while Anastasia was getting his hair cut in Jimmy's barber chair, a neatly clad gentleman stepped into the shop, drew a pistol from his vest and emptied it into Anastasia. The American Mafia had lost one of their founders.

No such protocol was in place when Jimmy Costello gave me my first haircut. Clinton was a far more innocent town and I was two years old. I was also scared out of my wits—so much so that I peed in his barber chair. Forty years later, Jimmy never missed an opportunity to remind me of that incident.

Jimmy was the most gregarious fellow one might ever hope to meet. In his day an icon of Clinton, I loved him and he loved me. If only my bladder had held up a little better. Sorry, Jimmy!

THE GOOSE THAT LAID THE GOLDEN EGG

Who remembers Golden Books? It's been a long time since I was two, so who knows if they are even published anymore? They were a reading mainstay for those perhaps too young to even read. They offered one didactic tome or another including the proverbial Goose that Laid the Golden Egg. My sister, Sue, read this story to little me hundreds of times, if she read it once.

The reason for the repetition? She would no sooner finish reading it to me when, in a burst of enthusiasm, I would plead with her to read it again. And again.

It so happened that a farmer went to his barn one day and, to his everlasting pleasure, found that his goose had laid a golden egg. Geese, of course, do not lay just one egg. Certainly there would be another tomorrow and another the following day.

The farmer, however, was unable to contain his greed. Surely, he reasoned, the goose had to be chock full of these eggs. Before word got out about his goose, he resolved to slay his goose and collect all the golden eggs at once. When he killed the goose and splayed it open, there were no golden eggs. Not even one! The farmer had killed the goose that laid the golden egg.

The lesson here for little, fragile eggshell minds is obvious. I get it. Thank you, Sister Sue for your incredible patience.

I wonder how Golden Books would survive today. Wouldn't the ASPCA be looking to shut them down? Or maybe DFYS (the Division of Youth and Family Services)? The nerve! To kill a goose only because it laid a golden egg. And how about the impressionable minds of our youth? Golden Books probably wouldn't last a year in today's climate!

OF GRIT, GRAIN AND GIZZARD

Leghorns are a bit impetuous, a little jumpy. The farmer can make a sudden movement at one end of the chicken coop and the hens' startled cackling will reverberate all the way to the other end. Within seconds, however, they're all calmed down once they realize there's no need to get riled.

As a tiny kid, I would be mesmerized by a coop full of Leghorns. It was a sea of white with a collective din of cackles. Wall to wall chickens seemed almost magical. Then at night they would roost, hundreds of them, stone silent 'til dawn.

Morning feeding was routine. First, and most importantly, water. Then mash: ground corn and other grains. Mash made for healthy, egg-producing hens. Next, "scratch." Scratch was cracked corn and other half-milled grain scattered on the floor of the coop, or on the ground if the chickens were "free range." With their talons, chickens would scratch the floor or grass to expose their next peck.

That should about finish the morning chicken feeding, wouldn't you think? Well, not quite. One last little detail still remains. Just do a quick check on the supply of oyster shells and grit. They're over in the corner in a little dispenser. The chickens can peck at them any time they want.

All right, wait a minute. Time out! Grit? As in ground granite or pebbles? Oyster shells? As in actual oysters? You're calling this chicken feed?? What's up with that?

Well, it's really pretty simple. Remember, chickens have no teeth. Not to get too basic here, but chickens can't chew. However, nature provides them with a stomach of sorts, called a gizzard.

The chicken also has the sense to swallow an occasional pebble, as in ground granite. The pebble migrates to the gizzard where there are other pebbles that the chicken swallowed a while ago. The everyday motion of the chicken moves the granite in the gizzard, effectively grinding food to a digestible consistency.

The chicken also senses substances containing high levels of calcium, such as ground oyster shells. It swallows them, also. Calcium is necessary to make eggshells hard.

But you knew all of this stuff in the first place, didn't you? Well, be that as it may, I might suggest that you pay humble homage to the hen. It's a more intricate creature than one might think. For it innately knows how to produce a nicely nurtured eggshell and how to keep its gizzard in good, grinding condition. Hail to the hen.

ONE LONG ROW TO HOE

As if keeping a dairy herd wasn't enough work at Tuckaway, one might have thought, from the size of our vegetable garden, that we were growing for an army. By canning, jamming, freezing, pickling, etc., Mom was simply ensuring that all this food would last the year long.

It was routine to sit down to breakfast, lunch or dinner with everything on the table being from the farm excepting the salt and pepper. This included any and all meats, all vegetables, milk, bread, butter—the works! Not that we didn't have a robust strawberry patch, but wild blackberries and wineberries that grew at wood's edge made enough jam to last at least a year on Mom's toasted homemade bread. She baked six loaves every other day.

What amazes me looking back, is that this was, as far as we were concerned, normal. As I contemplate it now, especially in the context of today's America, it was in truth far from normal. It was most unusual, but that never occurred to me as a kid. How did Mom and Dad do that? Well, it didn't just happen; we had a few well-worn hoes.

STRAWBERRY SHORTCAKE FOREVER

When you whip actual, real cream, not from a can but from a cow, you reach an immediate conclusion. The Reddi stuff that squirts from a container is a pathetic—with a capital P—imitation. Real whipped cream was a pivotal part of one of my sweetest childhood memories... strawberry shortcake. I have to assume that it is abundant in Heaven.

Mom's homemade biscuits were heavenly, as well. Crumble one up on fresh strawberries from the garden, add real whipped cream and the resulting shortcake was borderline indescribable. Addictive, but without harmful side effects, aside from maybe a little weight gain.

How could one feel negatively about weeding the strawberry patch when this was the result? We weeded like peasants, but we ate like kings!

JUNKEY AND ONION SEASON

I named the bike Junkey, for reasons that you may easily guess. Junkey was a bicycle's answer to a Sherman tank. Big and bulky, awkward to ride, no photos survive except for the one in my mind's eye. We didn't have a camera in those days, anyway.

Junkey suited a rough and tumble farm kid. The bike was heavy and rugged, having fat tires and an odd, spring-loaded suspension arrangement for the front wheel. When I wasn't milking cows, Junkey and I spent a lot of time together, even though the suspension rig only made it heavier.

Those of you not familiar with dairy farming may not know about "onion season." Wild onion, that is. It grew rampantly in the springtime pastures for a couple of weeks. When cows eat it, guess what? Essence of onion taints the milk! But if the critters chomped on hay for a few hours before milking, the onion taste would work its way out of the milk.

That's where Junkey and I came in. Each school day during the dreaded onion season, I would pedal Junkey three miles to Alexandria Township School. There's nothing like a little workout before school, especially since morning milking lasted 2½ hours before the ride. At lunchtime I'd pedal him back to the farm, call the herd into the barn, stanchion them and feed them some hay.

Lunch period dictated that time was of the essence. The ride back to school was as rigorous as the ride from there. Both had hills. Not to date myself, but this was well before the advent of the ten-speed bike, which would have made the whole routine easier. Oh well, no sense crying over spilled milk.

Needless to say, at the end of the school day Junkey had to be pedaled back home. Evening milking awaited. Not to mention, this whole routine had to be repeated the next day. Readers might understand why I was so happy to see the end of onion season!

I do not know whatever happened to Junkey. I'm sure he weathered his days to a rusting conclusion in an Alexandria junk pile somewhere. But he was one helluva bike, back when bikes were bikes. Plus, A&P never sold any onion-ated milk on account of Tuckaway Farm. Mission accomplished.

A CRUEL JUXTAPOSITION

Tuckaway's dairy barn wasn't a great distance from Mitchell's swimming pool, surely within earshot. Our beer grains pit was attached to the barn. I basically owed my soul to the beer grains pit. I shoveled tons of the stuff every day. The pit stunk, but beer grains made milk.

While I labored at this daily, sweaty duty, I could hear the raucous fun being had as the Mitchells and their friends splashed in the pool. I was hot and sweaty; they were cool by the pool. Sure would have been nice to be swimming with a couple of those Mitchell girls. They were becoming quite attractive little ladies.

Now, I don't want to sound self-pitying here. I had long since accepted that life wasn't always fair. I simply couldn't help but imagine, if only for a day, a little role reversal. What if one of the Mitchell boys was up here slinging this wet gruel into the feed cart while I was down there doing cannonballs in the pool? With the Mitchell girls?

That never happened, but at least I could entertain myself with the notion.

ED SULLIVAN - TV MAKES THE SCENE

Not long after the move to Tuckaway, Grandma Schanze acquired a nifty new invention, a television. Of course, never having seen one, we were abuzz with curiosity. On occasion at night, we'd go over to Capoolong to watch. Our visit was normally timed with the airing of *The Ed Sullivan Show*, one of TV's earlier variety programs. Ed Sullivan had virtually no talent himself; in fact, he was one of the most droll and odd personalities ever to grace a TV screen. A former entertainment and sports columnist, his TV career actually began in 1948. By the time we were watching him, he did have on quite the variety of talent during his hour-long show. I mean, who would not want to see Dean Martin, The Beatles, Milton Berle and the Balancing Bambino Brothers all in one hour?

I have long since perfected a fairly spot-on impersonation of Ed Sullivan. If sometime you'd like to hear my introduction of ZheZho ZhoZho and The Marquee Chimps, all you have to do is ask. I just can't promise that it will still be in black and white as all TVs were back then.

RAWHIDE AND *THE FLINTSTONES*

Mitchells had a swimming pool. We didn't.
Mitchells had a TV. We didn't.
Never was there even a hint of dissent between any of us, parents or kids, about what we had or didn't have. In fact, Mitchells were always more than gracious about sharing what they had. A Friday night tradition developed among Dave, me and the Mitchell kids that was great fun for all of us. Dave and I went down to Mitchell's house every Friday night to watch *Rawhide* and *The Flintstones*.

The *Rawhide* storyline revolved around men on a cattle drive somewhere in the old West. A young Clint Eastwood made his acting debut on this show. He played Rowdy Yates, the ramrod. How many of my readers, I wonder, know what a ramrod did on a cattle drive?

At any rate, as a kid, it appears as though I just couldn't get away from those cattle.

Of course, everyone knows of the iconic Flintstones. But here is something that maybe not everyone knows. The show often evoked the name of someone famous, but somehow worked the word 'stone' into the person's name. For example, actor Rock Hudson was dubbed Rock Hudstone.

I have already herein noted the name Ed Sullivan. For $64 then, what was his name on *The Flintstones*?

TRAFFIC ON THE BROOKLYN - QUEENS EXPRESSWAY

A dusty old radio sat on a shelf in the barn. It was eternally tuned to the same boring station for ages, WOR Radio in New York City. Every morning milking, without fail, we had to listen to *Rambling with Gambling*. Sorry, John Gambling; I, for one, grew to despise you! Your useless gibberish became the bane of my existence.

To add insult to injury, every ten minutes the station took you up to Flyin' Freddie Feldman in Helicopter 7-10 for an NYC traffic report. There I was, in my Carhartts and work boots, feeding chickens, slopping pigs and milking cows in the Middle of Nowhere, N.J. Why on Earth did I need to know how the traffic was doing on the Brooklyn-Queens Expressway? Or the Throgs Neck Bridge, for that matter?

I was about as far as I could get from there, in body and soul. Traffic finally eased up, as it most predictably would. So, why were we listening to this?

HAYMAKIN' BLUES—MAKE NO PLANS IN JUNE

When I was young, we not only made the hay on our own farm; for a while there, Dad was trying to custom bale the whole township. This was after we'd sold the dairy herd, so Dad was hell-bent on making the farm still pay. This, of course, was with an underpowered tractor, an ancient and temperamental baler and other equipment that were always on the cusp of breaking down.

Nonetheless, there were days when we would produce eight hundred to a thousand bales. Doing it the way that we were, thousand-bale days were exhausting. My, how things have changed! I know farmers in the neighborhood these days who make hay on a thousand acres a year and produce thousands of bales per day without touching a single one.

In later years, Judy and I only made the hay on our own farm. That was more than we needed. Most times we were lucky enough to have friends or neighboring kids who would help. Haying helps you find out who your friends are. The appeal wears off a hayfield in a hurry.

It's a simple concept that I struggled to make hay volunteers understand: we make hay when the sun shines. Getting close to hay season, our helpers would frequently inquire as to when we'd be baling. Bless their souls for their enthusiasm, but I would often get a blank look when I answered this perfectly understandable question with a perfectly understandable answer: "We're making hay when the sun shines." Cliché or not, it's true.

I never know exactly when that will be. And no, believe it or not, I have no special influence with the man upstairs. I need three straight days of sunshine to make hay, and I can't tell you, my good friend, just when that will be. The best I can say is that it will be in late May or early June. The weather is still unsettled. No, I can't adjust the baling hour around a helper's work schedule. I can only say I'll be baling when the hay is cured. I'll give you a call.

Does that sound a bit vague? Well, thank Heavens that we had helpers who finally understood the whims of Divinity. We got the hay in the barn.

I'm sure that I sounded like a broken record to Judy and the kids. It's June, for Heaven's sake. Don't schedule things that are not imperative. Help is needed in the fields and in the haymow and, no, I'm not sure exactly when.

THIRD BOX CAR, PITTSTOWN TRAIN

It was 1966 and it just wouldn't rain! Certainly it was the most severe drought that anyone had experienced in Hunterdon County. Nothing would grow unless heavily irrigated, but that became against protocol. Wells ran dry. Brooks stopped flowing. Ponds evaporated. Pastures were toast. It was seriously bone dry.

I think it was Cal Wettstein, may he rest in peace, county agricultural agent, who finessed a deal with a farmer's co-op in Indiana. The greenest, most beautifully cured alfalfa hay started rolling into Pittstown by the forty-ton boxcar. Yes, this was the same railroad on which were hauled the untold myriad of peach baskets during Hunterdon's peach heyday, but now that railroad was saving us. Indiana was saving us! There was no way farmers would survive without help from somewhere.

Now all we had to do was get the hay from Pittstown to Tuckaway. The railroad bosses gave us two days to do it. That would be twenty tons a day. Piece of cake? No way. It meant that Dave and I would have to take two days off from school to haul hay. It also meant that Distelfink would have to hold up.

She was, as best I can recall, a circa 1930 Dodge farm truck that had seen better days a long time ago. But she was all we had, so Distelfink would have to do, road-worthy or not. She was a flatbed and would carry a healthy load, provided that she could be kept running. So, off we trucked to Pittstown where the boxcar awaited us.

In those days it wasn't unusual for farm kids to take a day or two off from school in circumstances like this. Tommy Hager did it all the time. Sometimes, as in this case, there was work that had to get done and couldn't be put off a day longer.

For the record, it wasn't as though these were vacation days for us. We had 40 tons of hay to get out of Pittstown!

Day One proceeded without incident. Indeed, we got about half the boxcar emptied. That is not to say that trips back and forth to Pittstown weren't a little disquieting. Distelfink did have a problem; her brakes had a mind of their own. We were never sure how many times they'd need to be pumped before they decided to work.

Dad got a tad nervous anyway, and the brake issues didn't help. He orchestrated a little plan in case Dave and I had to jump from a runaway truck. That, of course, made us a little anxious, too.

There were two stretches of decline on the road from Pittstown to Tuckaway. With Distelfink lugging a full load, Dad's bailout plan addressed those two most dangerous points first. Where on those stretches was the softest-looking grass? Would a brakeless, fully loaded truck be moving too fast by the time it got to the soft-looking grass to make a jump not worth the risk? Were any of us using a slide-rule?

Fortunately, we never had to jump from the truck. We got that alfalfa home, all 40 tons of it. That was good. At the time of this writing, we're both still alive to confirm this story.

DE-RAILED

One day the train came off its tracks at Jutland. What a mess! Tipped over rail cars were everywhere; a daunting cleanup job for the railroad crews. But, one man's tragedy is another man's opportunity.

The railroad ties on one side of the track were terribly chewed up by the steel wheels of the runaway train. All ties from this section of the track would have to be removed and replaced. Dad made a deal with the railroad to do the removal part. Easier said than done, however.

Dad's thinking was this: these ties would make excellent fence posts, and they were free for the taking. They were, however, monstrously heavy, permeated with toxic creosote, and they featured an occasional railroad spike with burrs not guaranteed to be dull... but they were free! Of course, we had to go liberate them from the rail bed. Yeah, some "opportunity."

This, of course, was an occasion to fire up old Distelfink, our flatbed truck. She was custom made for this hauling episode. She did have a mind of her own, never guaranteed to start—or stop, but that was just part of the adventure. We climbed aboard, got her going, and lumbered over to Jutland where we started picking up the ties.

I can't help but recall the cruel and unusual elevation of that truck's bed. Was there really a reason to make it five and a half feet off the ground? Oh, of course: to make it easier to lift two-hundred-pound railroad ties up onto it and stack them. Silly, creosoted me! Why did I even question?

Should I have written a letter to Dodge Trucks Corp. about that? Or should I have just gotten out of Dodge? Either choice would have availed me nothing. So, we dug up and hauled railroad ties 'til we were black in the face. Abrasions on our hands and arms burned with smeared creosote. But out of that episode, we got some fence built.

Occasionally I'll come across one of those ties still standing tall out of the ground at Tuckaway, fifty years after I planted them as a kid. This was supposed to be a fence separating two parts of the farm. Dad never had us stretch wire to those posts. Project abandoned!

Wistful thoughts on my part? No, but lucky for Dad, labor came cheap at Tuckaway.

HED ED ED ULT ED HED ED ED ULT ULT

This was our version of the noise that the old FarmAll F-20 tractor made when it was running.

I say when it was running. It didn't run every time that we needed it. We cranked it each time that we wanted it to run, but the F-20 had a mind of its own. Freezing weather never agreed with the F-20.

When were these beasts manufactured, anyway? International Harvester Corp. made them between 1932 and 1939. To their credit, some forty or fifty years after that, they were still being pretty widely used. The F-20 had a draft gear that was slower than a Percheron, but it could pull like a whole team of them.

Getting the sweet old thing started was a ritual. Cranking it was not an easy task. With any luck, two or three cranks would get it going... on a good day. The cranker needed to be strong, yet nimble. Nimble because after each crank, he had to dart from the front of the machine up to the throttle to manipulate it into a successful start. If that didn't do it, try again.

Maintaining a tight grip on the crank was essential. If it slipped out of the cranker's hand, he would certainly learn how much torque that crankshaft had on it. The crank handle would spin around so fast that any hand in its way was sure to be brutalized. Ouch was a much too gentlemanly word.

Indeed, the F-20 reminded one and all of one simple fact: how hard men worked to get their tractors to run.

MILK STRIKE

It was nothing new for dairy farmers to complain about the poor prices they were forced to accept from the creameries to which they sold their milk. It amounted to little more than subsistence money for their product.

But, truth be told, it boiled down to a simple function of a market: supply and demand. I didn't know squat about such things back then, and I wonder how much the National Farmers Organization knew, too. Nonetheless, the NFO called for a "milk strike" to shake things up. If all of a sudden milk processors weren't getting any milk, the thinking went, then farmers would be better positioned to bargain on price.

So, for a few weeks, most local dairymen turned the spigot on their bulk tanks and let their milk go down the drain! Brooks and streams ran white for a while, but how long could farmers hold out? Not long; they weren't exactly well capitalized.

The NFO strike was the buzz among dairymen for a bit, but they were no collective bargaining juggernaut. The strike couldn't last long and, ultimately, had negligible effect.

One memorable moment from the strike does come to mind. With other local dairymen, Dad marched in picket lines at a local creamery. Each farmer carried a protest sign. After hours of marching, neighbor Norwood Reid stopped. "Woody" flipped his sign around, showed it to Dad and said, "Hey, what does this thing say, anyway?"

The strike had a singular lasting effect on this farm kid: it was demoralizing. Out in the barn at 4:30 A.M., only to watch our product gush down the milk house drain... this wasn't working the way it was supposed to. Neither was the milk strike.

Milk prices were ultimately unaffected; back to supply and demand. Welcome to farming.

KNUCKLEBUSTERS

It was about as close to primitive farming as I ever got. In the early days, we milked by hand. We then poured the milk out of the pail and into fifty-gallon steel cans. These cans were heavy when they were empty. When they were full, you don't wish to know!

There were two types of milk can. The preferred kind had a rigid handle welded to either side. The other type was known as a "knucklebuster." It also had a handle to either side, but they were loosely attached by armatures on the can. This meant that each time the full can was lifted, the lifter got his knuckles pinched between the can and the handle.

You might find these cans in antique stores across America. You will find that the knucklebusters are more expensive. Why? First, the knucklebusters are older, more of an antique. Second, to pay homage to the poor souls with bloodied knuckles who lifted those cursed things for years on end all across America. They are the true heroes.

At any rate, these cans had to get to a processing plant, otherwise known as a creamery. To do that, the cans had to be lifted onto a truck. Easier said than done, especially if there was two feet of snow on the ground. Given that, no truck would ever get to our milk house. Winter was a constant process of one step forward and two back.

For example, full milk cans meant it was time to harness the horse. Then, of course, hook the harness to the sleigh. Then, lift the milk cans onto the sleigh. Then drive horse, sleigh and milk cans to the end of the lane where, with any luck, a truck from the creamery would be waiting. Rinse and repeat. And repeat. And repeat.

I guess that was four steps back, but, Lord knows, we did it... all to get a few knucklebusters to market. How colorful, especially our fingers.

NAVY SHOWERS

Now, when you have about 2,500 men on a wartime battleship, taking a shower becomes a brief procedure determined by the need to conserve water. For starters, no running the water if your body wasn't in the shower stall. When the sailor was ready to shower, he stepped in the stall, turned on the water, got wet, turned off the water, soaped up, turned the water back on, rinsed off the soap and turned the water off. Immediately! Shower finished! Towel off and step aside for the next sailor.

Sounds rather disciplined, doesn't it? That's because it was. Now fast forward 15 or 20 years. The battleship *Massachusetts* has miraculously transformed into Tuckaway Farm. Lieutenant JG, Clare Tucker is now Captain Tucker. Despite all the change, the shower protocol is still in effect. There is only one bathroom on this ship.

In fairness to Mom and Dad, the Tuckaway showering discipline was not as rigid as here described, but the term "Navy shower" was commonly evoked. If the whole family had to shower, indeed, the process needed to move along and hot water was at a premium. I almost think Clare liked it that way. Maybe it reminded him of the old days.

Yes, we all kept clean, but barely.

LET'S GO METS

"Can't anybody here play baseball?" the iconic Mets manager, Casey Stengel, once lamented in the dugout at the old Polo Grounds. He had reason to ask that question. In their early days, the Mets were almost comically hapless.

How did two farm boys (Dave and I), in the middle of Hunterdon County, New Jersey, ever become Met fans? The Mets were in Queens, for pity's sake! Well, when the team was cobbled together in 1962, all the glory of baseball shone on the Yankees. The Dodgers were long gone from Brooklyn. The Giants were gone to San Fran. The Yankees were the only game in town. In our minds, the Mets represented fresh blood in New York baseball. Why not root for the underdog?

This was not to take anything away from the storied Yankees. Their history was epic, with a World Series record second to none. Dad, being from Michigan, couldn't care less. Also, Hunterdon County was neutral real estate. Heck, if Tuckaway had been a few miles further south, we may have been—perish forbid—Phillies fans.

So the Mets took the field in '62 with a host of notable names on their roster: Choo Choo Coleman, two Bob Millers, Jay Hook, Marvelous Marv Throneberry and Rod Kanehl. If they now sound like baseball also-rans, that's because they were.

Another name on that roster, Gil Hodges, was representative of what the Mets were able to achieve years later; attract talent from other teams. Consider their prior pitching staff: Jerry Koosman, Dwight Gooden, David Cone, Sid Fernandez. Even Tom Terrific Seaver had inked with the Atlanta Braves before the Mets managed to steal him away.

In their 54-year history, the Mets have played in five World Series. The Yankees have played in eight since then. No, the Mets haven't kept the Yankees' pace, but they've been respectable. Rooting for them has been a practice in loyalty. It certainly hasn't been all lollipops.

FRESH AIR

Now, stretch your imagination a bit. This will be easier for some more than others, but we'll all get through it.

It's the mid-1960s. You are a pre-teen kid, poor, I repeat poor. You are of Puerto Rican extraction. You have never once left your neighborhood in Spanish Harlem at the upper end of Manhattan. Your next bite to eat is often what you've been able to slip into your pocket in a nearby bodega. Destitution lingers here.

Your neighborhood is rough, very rough. Street gangs are the way of life. Stabbings, shootings and murders are commonplace. Life isn't easy here. As a kid, you see things that a kid should never have to see. But a temporary respite is in the offing.

Your mom (Dad having long since split the scene) has made contact with an organization called The Fresh Air Fund. In a few days, you and one of your brothers will get on a bus and travel two hours from the Port Authority to live for a time with a family on a dairy farm in Alexandria Township, Hunterdon County, New Jersey.

This will be an area and an existence totally alien to you. You are being totally displaced from your everyday realm. You're a tough, street-wise kid, but you have no idea what to expect. You'd never admit it, but you're a little scared.

How's that imagination doing, reader? Hard to place yourself here, isn't it? That's because if you're anything like me, your background is nothing like the one just described.

Duke and Harry Perez got off the bus at Clinton Point. A "Fresh Air" person accompanied them to make a brief introduction to my folks, my brother Dave and myself. After that, the Perez boys were ours for the next two weeks. Imagine the dichotomy. First, there was the normal social ineptitude of kids that age, us as well as them. Then, there was the stark difference between our two worlds.

It was going to be a challenge to make this work. Brother Dave and I were simply trying to get the work done on the farm. Why were our parents adding this level of discomfort to the mix? Anyway, we chatted a bit on the way back to Tuckaway. The mutual basics, our brothers, sisters and the like, weren't anything unusual or different.

We all arrived back home. Then came the big question. Now that we were friendly with the Perez boys, what was going to be the first thing that we did? The answer quickly became clear: Do what was next in our day-to-day routine and just let the Perezs tag along. This wasn't summer camp. It was not ours to entertain these guys. Just let it happen. So we did.

I suppose it was a good thing that there was no such thing as PETA back then. So, for example, if your horse stepped in a groundhog hole while out in the pasture, the horse most likely broke its leg. Never mind shooting the groundhog. You now had to shoot the horse. Point being, it was time in our routine to check our line of groundhog traps. Tuckaway suffered from an epidemic of those damnable rodents in those days. They had to go!

The routine was simple: Walk to each spot where a trap was set. (Just to clarify, these were the now-outlawed leg traps. It seems that no one was worried back then about cruelty to groundhogs.) If, at any one of the five or six locations where we had a trap set we found one that was sprung, we simply grabbed the chain that was attached to the trap, then pulled the trap back out of the hole, complete with attached live groundhog. Proceed to step B.

Have no doubt about it. The groundhog, at that point, was terrified and furious, hissing and biting at whatever came within its range.

Step B was simple: Club the beast to death. We carried an old piece of iron pipe with us on the trap check journey. This was a rather unceremonious part of the procedure, but this wasn't about ceremony. It was about killing groundhogs. Then fling the dead groundhog well out away from the hole and re-set the trap. Yes, buzzards have to eat too.

Step C: move to the next trap.

Bear in mind, a few hours prior to this, Harry and Duke Perez had taken their first steps ever out of Spanish Harlem! Did I mention that this was an existence totally alien to them? But, to their credit, they took it in stride. At least, the ice seemed to have been broken between us.

With the trap line check finished, back up to the house we went. It was near milking time. The Perez boys were about to learn how that carton of milk back in the bodega got there in the first place. This was all so new to them. Out we went to the pasture to herd in the cows. They stood there in the barn, amazed, as the milking machines were strapped on.

How I would love to meet up with them again, now some fifty years later, to hear about their impressions of their first day on the farm. What memories might they still have? What was the most important lesson they learned? Were we as different to them as they were to us?

It didn't take long, though to discover commonality between us. We all had our stories. They too could fight like cats, and then be pals the next minute. They too could eat with a vengeance. It was an education for all of us. I guess maybe Mom and Dad knew what they were doing, after all. Make no mistake about one thing though. In retrospect, this was a mighty compassionate thing that Mom and Dad were doing, especially after learning more about life for the Perez boys in Spanish Harlem.

Duke and Harry told us stories about their gangs, stories about crime in their neighborhood, stories about stabbings. Was it any wonder that their mom wanted them out of there for a little while? Was it any wonder that the next year, Duke returned to Tuckaway with another brother and stayed for six weeks? These poor guys needed a break. Life for them on a sleepy old farm was a godsend.

Young kids are like sponges; amazingly adaptable. After two weeks, Duke and Harry had the farm routine down pat. We'd go check the trap lines with a different twist. They would ferociously argue over whose turn it was to do the dirty deed if we came to a sprung trap. A bit of a turnaround, it seemed. Two kids from Spanish Harlem liked life on the farm.

Rest their souls, I feel compelled again to thank my folks for doing the "fresh air" thing. Indeed, it was part of our childhood education. I believe that if families did this on a grander scale, we would all be much the better for it. That is not to say that all families would have to do it just the way we did. Some may want to leave the groundhogs out.

STOKES STATE FOREST

In all of our years of dairy farming, we took one family vacation. That may seem a bit meager, but that was the nature of the beast. You are absolutely beholden to a dairy farm. If you want to take leave of it for a day, or a week, you must have someone who can take your place.

As a kid I never really expected a vacation, but the one we took lasted for five days. I just didn't get it, though! Tuckaway was, and still is, in a rather rural location, half wooded, half open, with wildlife everywhere. It is lush with springs and brooks. It has a beautiful stand of timber and a couple of makeshift campsites.

Why on earth then, would we vacation at Stokes State Forest in Sussex County? It wasn't as though this was a change of scenery! It wasn't as though there was anything that was compelling about it.

But, now that I think about it, maybe there was. No, it wasn't a change of scenery that the folks sought. It was a change of routine; a desperately needed one, at that. The woods in Sussex, however, are not terribly different from those in Hunterdon County. When we got home, it wasn't as though anything had changed.

Did we all have a change in routine? You bet! Maybe next time, at least the Jersey shore? That was Mom's preference, but it wasn't to be.

ALL HANDS ON DECK

To lift a bale of hay, one has to be strong enough to get it off the ground. This is the sort of rudimentary conclusion that I drew while pondering what age I must have been when I started working on the farm. I do know that I was pretty darn small and was part of the family crew before I could have lifted that bale. You don't have to be a body builder to churn butter. So, I did little kid jobs.

Dad ran a tight ship. He was doing what he had to do to keep shoes on four kids and food in our bellies. He had been a Lieutenant on a WWII battleship in the Pacific. He knew about efficiencies in a work crew. He also had a second job. Lord, how that man worked! But when he said, "All hands on deck," be sure that he meant it.

Dad had a third job too. On Saturdays he delivered eggs up in the posher areas of Morris County; house to house delivery of fresh eggs and freshly churned butter. That sort of service is long gone, nowadays. On Friday nights we were busy getting him ready for his route. "All hands on deck!"

My older siblings and the folks all candled eggs. Brother Dave and I churned butter. On Saturday morning after milking, we'd load up Dad's station wagon and off the peddler would go. He wouldn't get back until late in the afternoon, but he had some cash in his wallet.

Some of you might be wondering, "OK, how do you churn butter? And what the heck is 'candling eggs'?" First, butter. At our disposal we had a lot of milk, raw milk. That meant we had plenty of heavy cream. Put the cream into a churn that rotates a paddle and, after a whole lot of turns of the paddle, *voila*! Butter! That's a simplification, but you get the picture.

Candling eggs? Well, for starters, we had about 500 laying hens in the coop. All eggs, even those that you buy today at the grocery store, are checked for blood spots, which occasionally occur naturally in eggs. But natural or not, they're not anything that most folks want in their omelet.

You see, years ago eggs were checked for blood spots using the light of a candle, thus 'candling eggs.' Each egg was put up to the light, providing sufficient translucence to detect a spot. For the record, and so as to not date myself, we candled eggs with the help of a light bulb.

So, Dad was ready for his weekly route. This was a study in how a farmer leverages his farm to whatever extent he can to scrape together a living. Use the resources available. Be an entrepreneur. Pay the mortgage.

At any rate, as the youngest in the family, I became part of the work routine in first grade, maybe second. Being the youngest had advantages and disadvantages. If the chore, for example, was chopping thistles, I got the short end of the stick. What's chopping thistles, you ask? There were scads of them— sharp, pointy thistles, not exactly good eating for grazing animals. They needed to be controlled as much as possible or they would overtake a pasture. No such thing as weed killer in those days.

We were a little on the poor side. We had a FarmAll F-20 tractor that you had to hand-crank to start. That, and a manure spreader, were the extent of our farm equipment. My point is, we had no mower. With a whole farm full of cow pastures, there were thistles growing everywhere. My two brothers and I would venture out with scythes. Well, we only had two scythes. The smallest kid (me) got a short-handled sickle. That's a raw deal when you're chopping thistles. Run your hands into one now and then and you'll know why. You always got too close to the thistle with a sickle.

We would always be shoveling one grain or another into burlap bags, preparing for the grist. Brother Dan was bigger and stronger, so I did the little kid stuff, like hold the bag open, ready for the next shovel full. With all this grain around, rats were a constant problem. Dan would lift his shovel and out would run a rat in any possible direction. A game would ensue: bash the rat with a corncob. Our aims got pretty sharp.

On one such occasion, a rat ran straight up Dan's pant leg! This was now serious. The rat got to the point where it most certainly did not belong. From the outside grabbing in, Dan squeezed the dastardly thing to a squealing death right there in his Carhardtts. It was an ugly scene. From then on, we stepped a bit more lively in the corncrib.

Next day we'd be bagging barley. That job didn't have us conjuring up any games. It was the filthiest job on the farm, cleaning gutters included. If you've ever seen a combine harvesting a field of barley, then you've seen a cloud of thick, black dust following the machine; it was the same thing when shoveling barley into bags. When finished, you looked more of African persuasion. I don't at all intend that as a racial slight; you were just plain black. But a newfound perspective was gained.

For years I owed my soul to the beer grains pit. About every three weeks a big dump truck would come to the farm from the Pabst Brewery in Newark. Into a concrete pit it dumped a load of steaming "brewer's grains," residual barley from the brewing process. It was wet, steamy and had a reasonably pleasant aroma. It's a good thing I was older and bigger by then because it was heavy. It was used as feed for the dairy cows, and I had the "pleasure" of shoveling it, many hundreds of pounds per day, into a cart that was then wheeled to each stall for the cows.

Did I mention that this stuff was wet? A couple of weeks after delivery, the odor of it went from reasonably pleasant to downright rancid. I can still smell it. The beer grains pit still owns my soul. It made milk, though.

But it wasn't all bad. I had one daily job that, to this day, remains ever gentle on my mind. It was milking time, maybe in spring or summer. The herd didn't automatically come up to the barn. They were too happy to lie basking in the sunshine, and wouldn't come in on their own. Somebody had to go get them. I'd walk across the farm, find the distant herd and yell "C'boss, c'boss." Slowly they'd clamber to their feet and start walking.

Aster weeds by the streambed came in handy for rounding up the herd. Grown asters are five feet or so tall. Break one off at the bottom, strip the leaves and the farm boy had himself a perfect whip. No lazy milk cow argued with an aster whip. The cows ambled to the barn for evening milking. The end of another day drew nigh.

HAMMER DOWN, MARK 'EM SOLD!

This was it! If ever there was an event on the farm that could be described as surreal, it was today's. I had occasionally pondered what it must be like. All of the animals, all of the equipment, the tractors, the tools, the mows full of hay—within a few hours, all of these things were to be sold and hauled away for good. The magic of an auction would yield momentous change for our family.

Trucks and stock trailers started coming down the lane. First, a couple of Amish men from Lancaster County, PA, with their requisite non-Amish driver. Then familiar local cattle dealers, then a host of dairy farmers, some familiar, some not, began filling in the bidding audience. If this wasn't a scene in local color, nothing was.

The auction at Tuckaway didn't take long. We sold only the cows, the milking machines and the bulk tank. It was over within a few hours, yet the whole event seemed to be suspended in time. That, I suppose, was because I was savoring each moment. After all, my life was about to change dramatically. In a game of Monopoly, the "Get Out of Jail Free" card was always sweet. This was far sweeter.

Fred Daniel, a Hunterdon County auctioneer icon, had supplied us with numbered stickers for each cow. After milking that morning, we slapped them on, one per cow. When it came time for the bidding to begin, Fred perched himself up on his pick-up and that old familiar auction chant began. It was music to my ears.

SOLD! The first hammer hit the block; the first cow was returned from the barnyard, back into its stanchion and cow #2 proceeded into the auction yard. The next SOLD took a matter of minutes. This was easy! Before long, the whole herd was sold.

When the bidding ended, farmers started to load their new purchases. By the end of the day, it was as if a wand had been waved. All of the milk cows were gone. For the first time since the early Capoolong days, at 5:00 PM, there were no cows to milk. I'd been doing this every day since I was old enough to work in the barn. Believe me, this was surreal.

The pace of the next day was something to behold. There was a little cleanup left over from the auction, but other than that we were almost looking for something to do. This would take a little getting used to. Easier days at Tuckaway were in the offing.

I felt a little hollow. I couldn't help but think of my brother Dan, because he had done the milking full time before he went off to school. I felt that he should be sharing this newfound freedom. But he was away at school. It seemed unfair. He had earned this. But, hey, were things ever altogether fair on the farm? Were they anywhere? We'd already been down that road.

As it turned out, there was no shortage of things to do after the auction. After all, Clare Tucker was still captain of the ship. It was never going to be altogether smooth sailing. The horse business wasn't too far off in the future, but if there was ever a notion on Dad's part that farming was going to be a necessary part of the child rearing mix, he surely got his wish.

SIBLINGS

RAINY DAY MISHAPS

There are days on anyone's farm when weather rules the roost. It was a weekend; none of us were in school. That, of course, was when the work really ramped up. Dad would have a list a mile long for my brothers and me while he was off peddling eggs.

But what if the rain was coming down in torrents? What if everything on that list was outside work? Ah, shucks; we just might have to take a few hours off. Surely there were a few hours of inside work that could have replaced items on the list. Why not just switch gears a little and pursue them? Are you kidding me? We were kids, not angels. It was playtime.

Why was it then, on those occasions when we "let our hair down," that something bad happened? Was it so diabolical that we had opted to shed our work boots for a bit? Indeed, the devil plays hardball.

Do you remember "Pick Up Sticks?" They were a test of nerve and dexterity. The "sticks" were like giant toothpicks: wood, all of equal length, maybe eight inches long, about as thick as uncooked spaghetti and sharply pointed on each end.

The player held the bundle of sticks vertically in a ring formed by his/her thumb and index finger.

Release the ring, let the sticks fall randomly to the floor, and then observe the resultant pile with intent to "pick up" each stick while not even minutely budging any of the other sticks in the pile. The degree of difficulty was obvious. Any player who goofed was eliminated. The laughter that ensued was just the point.

On one particular day, Brother Dave was the lucky player. He managed to place his hand, palm down, atop a pile of the pick up sticks. He not only punctured his palm but also rammed one clear through his hand; in one side and out the other. Having done so, Dave was a bit in shock on the way to the Hunterdon Medical Center. The game of Pick Up Sticks had suddenly become no laughing matter. The scene was actually quite grisly.

In the old days of primitive, battlefield surgery, a patient might have been given a stick to bite on so as to quell the pain. Though the humor may have been delicious, none of us had the nerve to offer Dave a Pick Up Stick to bite on, to get him through the agony of yanking that cursed thing back out of his hand.

I haven't checked any toy stores. Is it possible that they don't sell Pick Up Sticks anymore?

* * *

I'm not sure that another homespun rainy day game even had a name. If not, I would be willing to volunteer one, here and now. How about a game of NumbSkull? Dave and me wiled away some hours playing that one.

Despite my suggested name, this game may have been the first indication that we were both to become literary giants! After all, the object of the game was to determine who could jump over the highest stack of books. When we both cleared the hurdle, another book was added to the pile. Luckily, we only had one copy of *War and Peace*.

Would you think that one of us was eventually going to get hurt? Well, make no mistake. The stack was getting higher. Our living room wasn't overly spacious. A running start would have helped, but, at best, it was an even playing field.

I had to be the one to trip over the top book and tumble to the floor, not without first slicing my forehead on a door hinge. This, of course, prompted another trip to the hospital. A mere six stitches patched the damage.

By the time Mom and me got home from the hospital it had stopped raining. Whoever would have thought that it would be good to get back to work? Hey, at least it was dry... and not as dangerous as playing inside!

SISTER SUE GOT A RAW DEAL

Sister Sue, five years my senior, never had to work in the barn. Pretty sweet deal, right?

You might surmise that this was some sort of chauvinistic, gender-driven arrangement from a bygone era. Not so: Sue had allergies. Bad allergies. She would be a mess if she even got near the barn. Sue struggled with this condition all through her childhood and teen years. I felt sorry for her.

She made the best of it. Sue was always cheerful, the quintessential positive personality. It wasn't as though, given her altered role in the work detail, that she did not stay busy. Mom had a heavy load in the house. Sue was right there with her.

Sue added cheer to a household that needed a little here and there. What better instrument to provide a little levity than the accordion. Sue practiced the "squeezebox" 'til she had it down pat. On many an occasion where folks had gathered, Sue provided the music. Not to unduly stigmatize the accordion, but friends sure did respond well when Sue squeezed out the Beer Barrel Polka. I can still hear her playing it.

A BYGONE WINTER

Every two weeks my brother and I shoveled corn from the outside cribs into burlap bags in preparation for the grist truck. Our gloves were made of a thin cloth. You didn't need to tell us how cold it was in that corncrib. My brother could tough it out. He was older. But the tears would freeze on my cheeks before they hit the ground. That's what the temperature was. It was cold.

I suppose that today this would have been a clear-cut case for the Division of Youth and Family Services, but hey, back then lots of us youngsters were working hard farming. Winter was tough on everybody. Frostbite played no favorites. Winter taught us kids to toughen up. In these days of "everyone gets a trophy," I wonder what we have lost?

One thing I think we have lost is the taste of black strap molasses. The grist truck had a tank of it mounted on the frame. It made for sweet cattle feed. But never mind that. Over the roar of the grist, we'd climb up on that truck, wooden spoons in hand and dust whirling, hell bent on reaching as far down into that tank as our short little arms would allow. Twirling up a well-rounded spoonful of black strap became an art form. Man, was that stuff good! It almost made bagging that corn worth it.

There wasn't much time on the farm for frivolity. But back in the early 1950s when my folks bought our farm, they discovered a cutter that was stored up in the rafters of one of the barns. A cutter is a one-horse open sleigh with a single two-person seat. On occasion, Dad would harness Nevada, our utility farm horse, and separately take each of us kids for a ride.

Life on the farm often a process of one step forward and two back. One day Dad took my sister Sue for a ride. Nevada pulling the sleigh, as usual. It had just snowed. I mean it snowed. What a beautiful scene that was; horse and sleigh gliding over drifts of white, Dad and sister in tow. Then something happened. Lord knows what spooked Nevada, but he took off faster than buckshot out of the old ten gauge. Dad couldn't hold him. I don't think anyone could have held him.

It was a spectacle not to be believed. Nevada was no longer paying heed to Dad's orders. He took off cross-country. That horse barreled through drifts up to his withers. The sleigh was not tracking well, wobbling side to side like an ancient hay wagon with shot wheel bearings. Gripping the reins, Dad leaned over and yelled in Sue's ear: "Jump when you can!" She did.

Sue's choice of snow banks wasn't that good, but she had little choice. She went in headfirst, legs sticking out of the snow.

Dad bailed, too. Nevada rounded the turn in the lane and rifled into the stretch a driverless horse. He was finally brought to a halt by the steel bars of the bullpens. A horse with even half a brain wouldn't dare to broach the bullpens.

The sleigh was retired that day. Nevada's performance had put an end to a family tradition. The old cutter was hoisted back to its resting place in the rafters and wasn't taken down again until time came to sell it some fifty years later.

That was not long ago. My wife and I put an ad on Craig's List. We got a call from a clueless young couple in Hoboken. They wanted the sleigh as a Christmas present for a relative. I very clearly told to them the measurements of the sleigh so that they would have a clear shot at fitting it into whatever vehicle would meet us in Hoboken when we delivered it to them.

But they screwed up. The sleigh would have fit better into a shoebox. We offloaded it from our pick-up onto the street while the couple left in their little car to find someone with a bigger vehicle. In the meantime, don't be surprised by the looks you get the next time you're standing on a Hoboken street corner guarding an old sleigh. We had two other offers while waiting, but the couple soon returned with a larger vehicle and cash in hand to seal the deal.

We didn't have to sell that sleigh. We sold it only to start getting rid of items no longer needed. In retrospect, I believe we never should have sold it. It evoked memories far more valuable than the few shekels that we got for it that day.

ONE SMOOTH RIDE

Some folks are aware of our affiliation with Tennessee Walking Horses. Not long after we sold the dairy herd, Dad was looking for a way to make the farm continue to make money. The idea of buying and selling horses, especially a little-known breed in New Jersey, was a dubious notion. But Dad had his enthusiasms. Off we went, sister Sue, Dad and me, on a horse-buying trip to Tennessee.

When we returned, Sue decided that she loved the place so much that she packed her bags and left Tuckaway. She never came back from Middle Tennessee except to visit. This afforded Sue, Dad, our respective spouses, and myself a decades-long connection with the Walking Horse country. We've enjoyed it immensely. Jude and I even owned a farm there for a number of years. "Tuckaway South" had some spectacular views!

Very unfortunately the Walking Horse industry gave itself a bad black eye over the years. Several owners and trainers simply could not be convinced to abandon some pretty hideous training techniques they were employing to force their horses to lift their front hooves higher, all for the sake of the show.

This shameful practice was and still is so unnecessary; it gives a hugely talented equine breed a totally unfair rap. That stigma stuck to the horses. Walking Horses themselves are wonderful. The people have been stupid. Will the practice ever fully cease? I wish I knew.

To this day, we have a few Walking Horses in the pasture. By their very nature, they deliver a Cadillac-like ride. No techniques needed, but a saddle helps.

BELLA DONNA and DYNAMITE

Brother Dave and I were working horses one day. After a time we paused to give our steeds a needed break. We didn't want to get them too lathered up. Our mounts were both stallions, not always a good combination if the horses' temperaments do not blend well together. That had never been a problem with these two, so there we sat in the shade of Tuckaway lane, our horses maybe ten feet from one another while Dave and I "chewed the fat."

I was on Dynamite, a two-year-old bay stallion. Obviously, at that age, he had everything to learn about what was expected of him, but he was coming along nicely. Dave was on Bella Donna, older than Dynamite by a year or two. As a saddle horse Bella Donna was never going to be outstanding, but we would find someone to buy him.

Quite suddenly, and without any obvious provocation, Dynamite lurched toward Bella Donna. Dynamite's nostrils were flared, ears pinned back and jaw wide open, ready to take a bite out of Dave's horse. This all happened so quickly. There was no way that I could restrain Dynamite before he buried his teeth into Bella Donna.

One problem: Dynamite missed. He got a mouthful of flesh, all right, but it was out of Dave's leg. Dynamite's bite was so intense that he pulled Dave right out of the saddle and landed him on the dirt! Bella Donna galloped off, I reined Dynamite under control and Dave lay writhing on the gravel road, in obvious pain. How things can change in three seconds of time.

By their very nature, horses are not always kind to one another. Especially young stallions. In the wild, will they sometimes fight to the death? That question is answered with a question: Surely you've heard about survival of the fittest? At any rate, Bella Donna ran off, which would have been the result of most such contests in the wild.

In the meantime, what to do with Dave, who lay there with one ugly chunk out of his leg? Well, what else was there to do? As long as he could walk, he'd have to get up and catch his horse so that he could, at least, lead it back to the barn. That is exactly what Dave did, gingerly!

We never let this happen again, and had to write it off as just another character-building exercise that occasionally took place at Tuckaway. Dave still has the scar to prove it.

BLOOD BATH

It was raining hard at Tuckaway. It must have been Saturday, because Brother Dave and I were cleaning horse stalls. In the early days, we kept only three or four horses on the farm, and we only cleaned their stalls on Saturday.

We took turns emptying the wheelbarrow into a manure pile, maybe 150 feet from the stalls, getting increasingly soaked for each trip we made.

After Dave returned to the stalls with the empty wheelbarrow and we'd commenced to pitchfork another load, I burst out laughing. Dave had pulled an old leather cap out of his pocket and yanked it down on his head. It was probably one that had been buried in a box of bolts picked up at a farm auction somewhere. Who cared? It fit him.

But the cap was dyed red. Soaked with rain, the dye had started to leach out of the leather and dribble down Dave's cheeks, temples and neck. A makeup artist could not have done a more effective job! Dave's whole head appeared to be soaked in blood!

We kept working for a while, musing about this odd turn of events. Then Dave conjured up a truly diabolical idea: Let's play a trick on Mom. I would drag Dave, complete with embellished agony, into the house and beg for an ambulance.

We did just that. Dave's acting was spot on. Some of the dye dripped onto the kitchen floor. Mom was understandably fraught with anxiety, pleading for details as to what happened. It did not take long for us to start laughing. Mom was not pleased.

Did any of you ever try to pull such a joke on your poor mother? I would hope not. If you did, I will assume that you are ashamed.

BROTHER DAVE - ABSENT WITHOUT LEAVE

It was profoundly sad, I thought, when it happened. It was the quiet desperation of a ten-year-old kid. After all, Dave hadn't given me or Dan or any of us a clue that it was about to happen. I'm sure the psychologists have a technical term for it, but the bottom line for Dave was that he was sick of working. SOW Syndrome, let's call it.

So, was Dan SOW? Was I? Perhaps, given the wrath of Dad, we simply feared to express that sentiment. Perhaps, better than Dave, Dan and I understood that by expressing such feelings, nothing would come of it. What were we going to do? Conduct a work stoppage? Sell all animals tomorrow? Stop weeding the garden? Not bloody likely!

But Dave had a little more chutzpah than the rest of us, so here's the scenario: Dave and I had our marching orders for the day. It should here be noted that after morning milking, Dad went to his full-time job, so Mom held sway 'til he got home. Our day's orders made our hearts sink, but we had no choice but to get on with things.

We were to start scraping the barn, a huge barn with peeling paint on all sides. Preparatory to re-painting, all this old paint had to be scraped off. That barn never held paint. Years earlier, we had painted it and it was all peeling again. To us, it was folly.

After laboring at this useless (to us) task for a while, Dave became agitated. He threw down his scraper tool and declared that he was done. He was leaving and wasn't coming back. He was sick of working! He walked over the hill behind the barn and disappeared from sight. He'd run away.

What were Dan and I to do? This was new territory for us. We laid down our tools, hustled up to the house and reported to the second in command. Mom was a bit flustered, but concurred with the plan we'd devised. Dan would saddle his horse, Nevada, and I would proceed on foot. We headed toward the woods in the direction where we saw Dave disappear. A regulation search party.

Surely he couldn't have gone too far. He had no food with him and no water, which served to indicate that he had no plan. Dave was probably just blowing off some steam somewhere.

I will pause to make a point or two here. This wasn't the first time that an impetuous kid ever ran away from home. That happens every day, but I was taking mental notes here, even as a kid. When I had kids, I didn't want there to be a reason for this to happen. This was nuts! Things weren't proceeding here the way they should.

It's all well and good for a kid to make notes such as this, but beware of the grip that your own childhood experience has on you. It may not be as easy as you think to change the patterns that are today part of your very being. Still, it's good to keep them in mind.

After a short while I heard a rustle in the bushes. I saw Dave duck back into the underbrush. "Here he is," I yelled to Dan, pointing like a bird dog. Dan galloped over on his horse. In seconds Dave was "apprehended." As expected, he swore that he wasn't coming back. I shut up and let Dan do the negotiating. Dave was seriously agitated.

He sought assurances that things would change, as though Dan held any cards. We all talked for a while, then, brothers to brothers, resolved to walk back home. You've heard of the Bretton Woods Agreement. This was the Tuckaway Woods Accord.

When Dad got home, I'm sure it was a seminal moment in parenting history. I have to imagine that Mom and Dad had a dead serious talk about what had happened earlier that day. I fully expected that Dave would incur the all-too-familiar rage of the Old Man. As it turned out, there was nothing. Not a peep! I'll bet Mom put her foot down.

I wished to never see a day like that on the farm again, and I'm happy to report that I never did.

THE JUAN VALDEZ OF TUCKAWAY

Many moons ago, you may recall a television ad that evoked a dirt poor farmer nestled deep in the Andes Mountains. His name was Juan Valdez. Juan had little in life but a well-worn hoe, but what did that matter? He grew the best coffee beans in the world... and the world knew it. Juan Valdez was a humble icon of discerning coffee drinkers on every continent.

Enter Dave Tucker, a not so humble, not terribly discerning hemp grower with visions of super-weed that filled his days. Much like Juan, Dave would pay early morning visits to his field and swell with pride at the progress of his crop. When harvest time came, this would be one smokin', profitable venture.

But, trouble was in the offing. Occasional campers from nearby Camp Tecumseh, run by the Salvation Army, would rove through the woods and make their way to Tucker Lane. These were innocent strolls in the forest, but they happened to be coincident with some pillaging that had taken place in Dave's hemp crop.

It should be noted that none of these campers ever did their wandering armed with machetes. It was true, however, that their strolls would have taken them near Dave's crop, and yes, someone had hacked at Dave's hemp. Circumstantial evidence, at best.

Well, never mind innocent until proven guilty! With amazingly little forethought, Dave saddled a horse and rode into Camp Tecumseh. He advised camp officials as to the nature of his nearby crop and the recent proximity of some of their campers. Further, he informed them that his field had recently been plundered and that he wanted this to stop. One is reminded of the age-old question, "Are you stoned or are you just stupid?"

Well, months went by without incident. The crop was harvested and hung like so much tobacco in a nearby barn to dry. There it awaited local legal personnel to show up and do some plundering of their own. Indeed they did, and it was a bust of dramatic nature.

Word of the sordid goings-on down the lane filtered to Clare Tucker. He phoned Dave's abode. Dave, at the time, lived in the current Ennis house further down the lane. Charlie Mann lived with him. Charlie fielded Clare's phone call.

"Charlie, what the hell is going on down there? I've been drinking bourbon all afternoon, just trying to figure out what to do about you guys!"

It was a dubious way for Clare to frame his question, as if he was trying to bridge the generational gap. Yes, bourbon was his hemp, but things were getting out of control down the lane. Things better straighten out!

There hadn't been this much excitement in this neck of the woods since the still got busted many years prior. One wonders whether Dave Tucker continues his errant ways. I will defer to my readers to venture a guess.

DAN BORE THE BRUNT

From Capoolong to Tuckaway, brother Dan worked harder than all of us. I suppose that was simply a function of being first born, but it was more than that. Getting started is always the hardest. Dan and Dad worked tirelessly just to get the barn at Tuckaway ready for milking cows before Dave and I were even in the mix.

Part of Dan's daily routine was cleaning gutters, all by hand. Tough physical work it was and the dirtiest, sloppiest job of the whole day. He handled it with a sense of humor, though. After getting swatted in the face with a urine-soaked tail, it helped to find whatever glimmer of levity the circumstance might afford, and Dan would find it!

We were working in a field one morning on a hill. Dan was driving our little Ford 8N tractor. Dave was sitting on the fender. Dan braked to stop. Slipping on the dew-covered grass, the tractor kept moving. With Dan's foot still on the brake, the tractor quickly gained momentum and slid all the way to the bottom of the hill, finally coming to a stop.

Without skipping a beat, Dan very calmly turned to Dave and said, "Well, Sport, looks like we have a runaway tractor on our hands."

Dan's unflappable nature and sense of humor certainly served him well as a ship Captain many years later. Maritime college had undoubtedly made for intense military training, but Dan joked about it. Fort Schuyler wasn't so bad, he would muse.

"At least you can sleep in 'til reveille!"

DAN FLIPS AN M

The FarmAll M was an iconic farm tractor manufactured long ago by the old International Harvester Corp. Farmers surely had their preferences, and prejudices, when it came to tractor models and tractor manufacturers. They would banter back and forth about tractor models the same way eighth graders would about Fords and Chevys.

That's about all it was – banter. The fact of the matter was, back then America was manufacturing the world's best farm machines, hands down.

There were millions of FarmAll Ms across America's heartland. Like any tractor, they had their good features and some that were not so good. The M was a "tricycle tractor," not so good. Its two front tires were coupled closely together, a "narrow front end," meaning that the machine essentially had a single contact point on the ground at its front.

Now, before I bore you stiff with the mechanics, I only ask that you imagine how this arrangement might make for less stability, less balance of the machine. But wait: there was further peril.

Danny Baker, rest his soul, owned what is now the Swift Farm (rest Mr. Swift, also) on Rick Road. On this one particular day, Danny was hell-bent busy baling hay. My brother, Dan Tucker, then in eighth grade, was working for Danny.

Needing to get a tractor from the field where they were working back to the farmstead, Danny put Brother Dan on the seat of his M tractor, jammed it in 5th gear and sent him on his way. Brother Dan was not at all familiar with an M and surely didn't need to be going that fast.

The trip took Dan down the slope into Mt. Pleasant where there was a sharp left turn onto Rick Road. With plenty of loose gravel on the road, the M didn't handle the turn. Its front tires skidded; the tractor flipped over and blew up in a fury of flames thirty feet high!

Dan could easily have been killed, but he was incredibly lucky and escaped with only a few cuts and bruises. The incident, however, was a reminder that despite the frenetic pace of farming in the summertime, we all needed to slow down a little. It's a wonder that there aren't more tragic accidents on farms. As it is, there are too many.

Funny how Dan "forgot" to tell Dad about the accident. Later that evening, however, Danny Baker phoned the house to inquire as to Dan's well-being. With the cat out of the bag, Dan acquiesced to Dad's questioning. Dan assured him that he was OK. Dad, in his usual compassionate tone, said only one further thing.

"Well, ya' damned fool! Why didn't you clutch at that corner? You could have been killed!"

Surely Dan was already aware of that.

MIND YOUR MANNERS

In high school, Dan read Herman Melville's book, *Moby Dick.* The story had a lasting effect on his life. He decided that he wanted to go to sea. When the time came for college, he attended New York State Maritime College at Fort Schuyler in the Bronx. Scholastically, this was going to be a challenge.

At the end of his first semester, Dan had pulled down some pretty good grades. Mom and Dad decreed that the family would go out to dinner to celebrate Dan's achievement, at The Union Hotel in Flemington.

At the risk of sounding a little redneck, Mom preached to us kids for a week about brushing up on our table manners. We were reasonably well schooled in that regard already, but the fact was, we'd never been out to dinner. Mom was a little concerned that we might prove to be an embarrassment.

The big night came. Mom, Dad and all four Tucker kids were out on the town. This was a rarity. The night before, there was a huge snowstorm. On the way to Flemington, I recall riding through someone's barnyard to get back on the road. The snow was tunneled on both sides of the road, well above the roof of the car. But, we made it to the Union Hotel!

We ordered our meals without incident and the first course was served. Right away Mom bungled the handling of her spoon and proceeded to spill fruit cocktail all down the front of her blouse. Talk about an embarrassment. Talk about redneck... from Miss Manners, herself.

We never were a family that held back when it came to poking a little fun at each other and, most certainly we did not on this occasion. Mom never heard the end of it. It became part of our family lore. Mom took an innocent slip of her fingers to her very grave but we all had a lot of fun with it.

ANIMAL STORIES

QUEEN COW DID IT!

I couldn't have been more than three years old. Mom was out working in the barn and, because I still needed to be watched, she had me out there with her. The cows were coming into the barn from outside, each walking to her habitual stanchion. Mom would then lock each stanchion, cow enclosed.

A cow named Queen started to enter. I must have spaced out a bit and managed to be standing right in the aisle where old Queen had to walk to get to her stanchion. This spooked her a little and her reaction was to just put her head down, keep walking and... well, yes, bull me right over! Damned Guernseys.

I suppose that I was lucky. Queen only stepped on me once, but that was on my head! I bled like a stuck pig. Mom promptly got me out of the way, locked Queen's stanchion, then hurried me up to the house to get me straight into the tub. While Mom was stripping me of blood-soaked clothes, I was bawling hysterically.

Now, remember, I was all of three years old. I had no great command of the English language. As I sobbed and drew breath for my next shriek, I kept repeating one simple, sentence: "Queen cow did it! Queen cow did it! Queen cow did it!"

Ever since, I am occasionally reminded of my Queen cow proclamation, as though there was ever any doubt who did it! Certainly through my childhood I was reminded of Queen, every time I sat in Jimmy Costello's barber chair.

You see, my brothers and me used to get butch cuts. I mean, we got shorn like so many sheep. This, of course, laid bare the nasty scars from my Queen cow incident. Was there ever any doubt that Queen cow did it? Look at my butch cut!

BIG, DUMB DORA

Dora was an inordinately tall cow, even for a Holstein. The herd could have been grazing a great distance away, but Dora was still identifiable among them because she stood head and shoulders above the pack.

Dora was so big that she wouldn't even fit into a standard stanchion. We had a separate box stall for her in our dairy barn. It would have been one thing if, after this special treatment, Dora was an exceptional dairy cow, but she wasn't.

It should be noted that just because she was tall, Dora did not have a soaring bovine intellect. In fact, our common term of endearment for her was Big, Dumb Dora. Cows never seem to be terribly clever, and Dora was no exception.

Once, in the dark of night, one cow in the herd found enough of a breach in the fence to be able to wriggle her way to freedom. Of course, a second cow had to join the first. Shortly, the whole herd was out. The cows found their way to the nearest neighbor's house, but there was no neighbor there. The place was abandoned.

It is always unsettling to a dairy farmer when he ventures out to milk in the pre-dawn dark and his herd is nowhere to be found. In this case, his first chore of the day is, obviously, to find them. Needless to say, that chore is rendered more difficult without daylight.

With ears cocked, we soon detected the subtle lowing of cows. The whole herd was milling around the nearby house. First light, as the sailors call it, was by now aiding our eyesight. We started rounding up the herd and heading them down toward their barn.

There was an empty swimming pool on this property, 4 feet deep at the shallow end, 8 at the deep. Dismayed, we heard a moo coming from its depth, but we had to get the rest of the herd up to the barn before we could attend to this complication. All our cows took to their accustomed stanchions once we got them to the barn.

So far so good, but which cow was still down there in the swimming pool? After taking inventory, we knew it was Big Dumb Dora. When we finished with milking we'd have to go get her. This would be a daunting task.

With milking done and in broad daylight, we walked down to survey the Dora dilemma. There she stood, seemingly unaffected, as though this was simply part of her daily routine. One would have thought, after falling at least four feet, maybe eight, onto a concrete floor that Dora would be injured, but she appeared to be unscathed. She stood there at the bottom of the pool and stared at us, as if to question our next move.

This was going to take some engineering. It wasn't as though Dora could get a running start and pole-vault out of the pool. Dad drove up to Paul Fritsche's place to ask him to come down for a consult. Paul and Dad talked it over. Pretty soon they decided that the best plan was to build a ramp for the cow. Dora just stood there.

Word soon spread that there was a "situation" down at Tucker's farm. Two other neighbors showed up. Marty Smisek drove back home to get some tools. Paul went back up to his place where he had a sawmill. We needed lumber. A half-day's work ensued and a ramp was built. Meanwhile, Dora just watched. She knew something was going on, otherwise, why all this activity in her pool?

Now, just because a ramp was built, there was no guarantee that the animal would willingly walk up it. It may have now been visually obvious to Dora that the ramp was her ticket out of the pool, but remember what we have already observed about Dora. At any rate, the time had arrived for Dora to escape from her captivity. Would she cooperate?

No. Not even close. It took four men, poking and prodding, screaming and yelling; Dora just planted her hoofs and refused to budge. A second technique of two big men cupping hands behind the bovine and inching forward finally succeeded. Eureka! Finally Dora stepped off the ramp and out of the pool.

I'm unsure if men did high-fives in those days, but certainly there was some such version. All neighbors involved in this episode were then able to return to their own day's work, almost as though they hadn't already started. Indeed, neighbors helped each other in those days. They had to.

Not long after, Dora was culled from the herd.

CALVING

I believe that I've painted this scene already, perhaps sparing my readers some of the gory details. Well, that's over; no more Mr. Nice Guy.

It may have been evening, but more probably was morning. It was nice of the herd to have set their collective biological alarm clock. They were not far from the barn at milking time. They didn't need to hear "C'boss" but twice to prompt their slow return into the barn. Were they all present and accounted for? Yes. All but Cora.

This, of course, was no surprise. Cora had been due to calve two days ago. She was so big last night that she could barely fit in the barn. Part of the routine for this farm boy was to go find calving cows, wherever they had wandered to on the farm. It might take a five-minute walk or considerably more than that. They always sought a spot to calve far from the rest of the herd.

There was reason for that, incidentally. Calving is not a community affair. Animals in general have some strange birthing rituals. One might think that the balance of the ladies in the herd would accommodate their calving sister. Actually, the opposite is true. A great deal of agitation is prompted by a newborn calf if the rest of the herd is in the immediate vicinity.

Cows, fraught with angst and curiosity over a five-minute-old calf, will actually injure or kill a newborn simply because the new calf isn't their own. With several of the herd milling around a birthing scene, I had witnessed some ferocious battles between the new and completely exhausted mother trying to protect her newborn from other cows.

Truth be told, I was Chief Herd Obstetrician only by default. Dad and my brothers were busy milking. This is not to say that one didn't need to know a little about what he was doing. I might have been all of ten years old, but I had already delivered more than a few calves. It was delicate business. It was dangerous business. I only had to learn once that some primal maternal instincts were at play here. Only once did I need to feel a horn brush by my temple to know that caution was the word. Besides, I was alone; it was no time to be getting gored.

At last I found her. There was Cora, to no surprise, lying down behind some wild wineberry bushes, well hidden. First step? Approach her gradually; talk to her as you do. Perfect, you haven't startled her. She knows you are there. Your slow approach has allowed you to make observations. She is laying flat out, head on the ground. You've gotten right up close to her now and she hasn't been spooked. You know your animals and know that that's not like Cora. She is otherwise involved!

She's broken water. She's in labor! Last year, as a first-calf heifer, she had a tough time calving. Typically, the second time around it goes easier. Fortunately, she is far enough into labor that human presence is not her first concern.

I kneel down to her back end. Good; no breech birth going on here. Front hooves and nose are just starting to appear. Now clear mucus and after-birth from the calf's nose.

Cora is working hard, but her calf has to start breathing. Let her work on it for a while and watch her progress.

Progress wasn't happening. Cora would push and strain, then do it again, but after ten minutes nothing much was happening. At least, keep the calf's nostrils cleared, then start helping her. Conveniently, the handles were provided.

I dried the calf's front hooves as best possible to secure a grip and timed my first pull with Cora's next push. After a few pulls, we might have gained an inch. She'd have to further dilate to get past the most difficult obstacle, the calf's head. This could take a while.

Soon Cora and I were both working hard. Progress was slow, but we were getting there. Cora was determining the pace. It made no sense for me to be pulling if I wasn't exactly in time with her pushes. One of these attempts would do it. Was my talking to her doing any good? Who knew? I just wanted to remind Cora that she wasn't alone.

Here came another contraction. A mighty effort on her part, a mighty effort on my part and whoosh—out came the head. The hard part was over. Cora knew it and I knew it. A few more tries and this calf would be on the ground. And so, after another couple of minutes, it was.

Shucks! It was a bull calf, but Momma was going to be okay. In a minute, Cora was up and licking her calf. That is another ritual that can take a half hour or so. My job was done. I was a sweaty mess with mucus in my hair, but a stream wasn't fifty feet away. Thank you, Cora, for making it so easy for me to wash up.

I'd probably been away for an hour. It was time to head back to the barn with a report. At this point, Dad would be worried. I would come back for Cora and calf before the herd was let out from milking. This way, there would be no confrontation between the herd and the new calf.

Oh, and about the calf being a male; that was just a little tough luck. A heifer would have stayed right here on the farm, part of the futurity team. A bull? On Tuesday, it's on a truck to Hackettstown auction. Surely you've heard of veal!

BREEDING CHART

A while ago I stumbled across a chart that hung in our dairy barn for many years; a chart that tracked breeding records of each individual cow on the farm. There it was, beginning in 1962, all in Dad's handwriting.

I was most amused by reviewing the cows' names; even more amused by the fact that I could recall details about so many of these critters more than five decades later. And, where did Dad come up with some of these names?

Lotus. Bambina (she was a Jersey). Suds. Augie. Duchess. Hermes. Babs. Della.

I recall the day when Barbara produced over a hundred pounds of milk between morning and evening milking. Think about that one! A hundred pounds in a day. I think that's called Lactose Corpulent.

Most other names were on the common side. Candy was another Jersey, along with Candace, her daughter. Wendy, Phyliss and Nora were milk cow mediocre. Suzie and Sally provided the alliteration. Yoshabelle threw the curve ball.

I guess Dad was trying to have a little fun with this. Why not? Farm humor belonged in the barn as much as anywhere. If we couldn't laugh at our hapless bovines and ourselves then what good were we?

CAT MAYHEM

Every dairy barn needs cats. Mice needed to be controlled. Rats too. A plethora of cats lived in the dairy barn at Tuckaway. None of them were 'fixed.'

Was it cold for them in the winter? Duh! It was cold for everybody. These inane SPCA commercials on TV miss one essential point. Millions of animals worldwide, wild or domestic, are amply provided by nature to stay warm, including cats. But, I digress.

Tuckaway's cats were well-fed, thanks to mastitis. What's that, you might ask? Each cow, prior to each milking, had to first be checked for mastitis, a mammary inflammation. Each quarter of each udder was checked by squeezing a squirt or two of milk into a small tin cup with a black insert atop of it, allowing sight of any clots in the milk. The 'strip cup' was then emptied into the cat's milk dish. The cats, therefore, got lots of milk.

At milking time, the cats stayed near their accustomed dishes at one end of the barn. Mom fed dry food to the cats at the other end, also during milking. The barn was L-shaped, thus a 90-degree turn between the two spots. Mom arrived with cat food and yelled out "Kitty, kitty, kitty, kitty."

This prompted an immediate stampede of cats to the other end of the barn. It was a sight to behold. Running full-tilt when they made the ninety-degree turn, none of them knew enough to slow down. Some would nearly flip over. The paws of others, mid-turn, would momentarily still be moving while the actual cat was not, like an animated cartoon. It was hysterical.

Why do I devote all this ink to describe something as mundane as the cat rally? Hey, I'm a simple guy; easily entertained! Milking was borderline monotony. We needed some levity here and there. We took what we could get.

Plus, it is a perfect lead-in to lend kudos to neighbor Chris Mitchell, Arlo's older sister. Not because she had to, but because she wanted to, Chris was in the barn for every milking. In fact, Chris was the self-appointed mastitis checker. What an added plus she was to the crew.

THE CALLOUSED CURS OF ALEXANDRIA

I am continuing to go way back. Our new neck of the woods at Tuckaway was remote, Spartan, if you will. Half-wild dogs tended to band together and roam the countryside. The longer they were on the loose, the wilder they became, like wolves or coyotes. No one tried to pet these dogs if they knew what was good for them.

You may ask, well what about the dogcatcher? Hey, the old, curmudgeonly dogcatcher was nowhere near a match for these dogs! He looked the other way, turned the other cheek to these roving canine mobs.

Although I was only three or so, I shall never forget one incident. Mom was letting the cows into the barn. They were in their usual single file saunter, each step as measured as the last. No hurry. The barnyard would still be there when they again stepped out to pasture.

Out of nowhere a wild dog pack appeared on the scene, maybe six of them, barking ferociously, growling and gnashing their teeth. Was any peace-loving cow going to challenge that? The dogs disrupted the whole routine, standing right in front of the barn door and blocking any further entrance.

Mom had to do something. Leaning against the barn wall was a piece of rough-cut 2x6. She grabbed one end, raised it over her head and swung a mighty arc with intent to deliver a staggering blow to the biggest dog. The dog, with lightning deftness, not only avoided the swing but also clenched the board in its teeth and wrenched it out of Mom's grasp!

Was it any wonder that the dogcatcher never challenged these curs? Fortunately, Mom's challenge left an impression on them. They at least got the idea that they weren't welcome. They dashed off just as quickly as they had arrived. It had just been another day in the frontier-like routine of daily living in Alexandria Township.

PIGS IN THE RIGGIN'

We didn't raise pigs for profit. There was no grand pig plan. The only plan was to put some pork in the freezer once in a while, and provide us with some comic relief. Pigs did just that. They happen to be funny.

Raising pigs was a piece of cake. They didn't need to be milked. (Hallelujah!) Their breeding didn't need to be monitored on some chart. They didn't need acres of fenced pasture. They just hung around in their pen and fattened up. They would grunt once in a while, then go back to sleep.

Pigs are not pretentious. They don't worry about gaining too much weight. In fact, they seem to understand that that is their job. If a pig is caked with mud because it's been wallowing in a puddle the day long, so much the better. This is Pigdom the way it should be. The pig just grunts and goes back to sleep.

It used to be that we gave each cow a name. That was for a reason. Managing the herd, it was necessary to identify each animal. If there were only two pigs, however, their names were more for giggles than specific identity. The two pig's names were sort of interchangeable. Prudence and Priscilla were almost one and the same.

We did assign some rather jocular names to our pigs. Sal and Manella, Samantha and Delilah and, of course, Rigor and Mortis. The pigs themselves didn't seem to care one way or another. They were aloof, lost in pig oblivion. They just grunted and went back to sleep.

I can recall only one occasion when our pigs escaped their pen. That is a fortunate thing. Even occasional pig escapes are not good. They don't herd well. They won't stand for anyone trying to put a leash on them. They run very quickly and they are extremely difficult to tackle.

On the occasion of the aforementioned escape, our pigs made the best of it. Their bid for freedom was protracted, but we finally cornered the buggers and got them back in their pen. They were a bit winded, but their next step was all too predictable. They just grunted and went back to sleep.

HOW NOT TO FIX FENCE

Keeping fences patched up was a constant job. If thirty cows busted through a fence and wound up over at a neighboring farm, it amounted to an unpleasant reminder that somewhere on the farm a little barbed wire needed stretching. The old adage about good fences making good neighbors held true. A bunch of stranger cows suddenly mixed in with your dairy herd wreaked havoc! Worse yet if those cows were ours.

It was never as though a new fence was made and then never looked at again. Critters always look for a means to scratch. They are heavy. They push things over. They wear things out. They try your patience. Or maybe a tree fell on the fence. On a farm, it could be any one of a number of things.

When the cows got out, a whole procedural chain was set in motion. First: Recon. Where on the farm was the breach? Would a new post need to be set? Is it a board fence? Is it a wire fence? What tools would be needed to fix it? Knowing the nature of cows, was further work needed on the whole stretch other than just the escape spot?

These were the weighty questions facing the workers tasked with fixing the fence: Dave and me. It was a small job that day, and shouldn't take too long. We wouldn't even need new barbed wire, but the repair was way out near the back of the Big Field. No problem; we'd just ride Dan's horse Nevada back there.

We had never tried it this way before, but why not? It beat walking. The tools we would need were minimal; hammer, a small bag of fence staples, wire stretcher, wire cutters and a hatchet.

Western saddles had those frilly leather laces hanging from them in abundance. Our plan was simple. Put those laces to a good use finally; tie the tools to the saddle. How else would we arrive at the job with the tools that we needed? We hoisted the saddle on Nevada and did just that. Perfect. There were just enough laces for each tool that we needed.

Dave mounted Nevada. I was going to walk behind, having opted not to ride double with him. That was a good decision, as things turned out.

Dave reined Nevada in the proper direction. The horse was nervous, sensing the extra accouterments on the saddle. When they began to jingle, Nevada went ballistic.

The horse bucked with a spirit I've yet to see at any rodeo. Tools went flying. Dave went flying, too. When Nevada finally calmed down, the driveway was peppered with tools and Dave was on his duff. The morning wasn't getting off on the right hoof.

We took off the saddle and put Nevada back out to pasture. We had certainly learned not to do that again. We fixed the fence that day the old-fashioned way: we walked to it tools and all.

CHILLIN' WITH THE PIGEONS

Yes, it was an admittedly odd method of escaping the daily grind, but I needed it sometimes.

Pigeons, a dozen or so, would roost in the top of the farm's silos. There they would sit in placid stillness. Occasionally, one would fly away. But, then another would fly back in, prompting a momentary stir among the flock.

But all the while—they're cooing. Their distant, mesmerizing cooing, fifty feet atop the silo. At bottom, I parked myself and would simply listen. The sound produced a fantastic echo in the empty silo, a lull, an invitation to rest.

These were relaxing "white noise" sound effects before there was any such thing.

Then, for no obvious reason, they would all fly away. Not to worry! They were one of the most consistent things on the farm. They'd be back.

I loved listening to these pigeons in the silo. They were a needed respite for a wearied farm boy before the work commenced again.

Grandpa Alfred Keyes Schanze, circa 1908

Janet Schanze seated, her sister Laura Jean on floor. Janet couldn't pronounce Laura Jean, so little sister became known as Laje. 1925.

The stone tenant house at Capoolong, covered with ivy. My Great grandpa Gillon helped to build this house in the twenties. He had been a stone mason in Scotland. I spent my first two years in this house. Circa 1975.

My mom, Janet Schanze. Best guess, 1942

The farmhouse at Capoolong, built prior to the Revolution. I have many fond childhood memories that happened in this house! Circa 1975.

Dad provides his bride-to-be no help over the barbed wire fence. 1945 at Capoolong.

Grade school photo.

When Jude and I moved in 1980, this four room bungalow (circa 1946) got a little tight for the five of us!

In Tuckaway woods, Dave sits on Mom's lap while Dad relaxes, puffing his ever-present pipe. I ponder how trees are such monuments to time! Circa 1959.

Pete Tucker

We were given a choice between getting a TV or getting a horse! We got a bonus, two horses! Chocolate and Vanilla. Dan leads Chocolate. Sue rides Vanilla. Mounted kids are me, Dave and (best guess) Chris and Alex (Sandy) Mitchell. Tuckaway, 1955.

A carefree me sitting on the yard fence at Tuckaway with a makeshift belt. One of the few remaining solo photos of me as a kid, the folks never having had a camera. Circa 1961

Tuckaway South view from the driveway, April 2011.

The Tucker kids, Dan, Sue, Dave & me, all dressed up at McClintock Studio in Clinton circa 1959.

From left, Dad and Mom, Aunt June and Uncle Bud Tucker at their home in Mt. Morris, Michigan. May 17, 1995.

'Summer House' at Tuckaway Bradford, Summer 1991.

Grandma Schanze folding clothes for "baby Danny." Capoolong, circa 1946.

The three sisters. From left, Aunt Laura Bailey, Aunt Evelyne Powers and Mom at Aunt Evelyne's apartment for her 75 birthday, NYC Feb. 21, 1987.

Mom and Dad at Tuckaway Bradford, November 7, 1995.

SCHOOL DAYS

KINNYGARDEN and THE COCKBIRD

Alexandria Township School (ATS), occupied the same building as the current Lester D. Wilson School, but it wasn't named as such in 1958 when I first graced those hallowed halls. Not that I remember that much from back then. Bear in mind, I was just entering Kinnygarden. Mine was a fragile, eggshell mind.

I'm curious. How much do you remember from elementary school? For starters, can you name all of the teachers that you had, grades K thru 8? I can. I can't remember much else, but I do recall each of their names. Much of the rest of grade school is pretty vague in my mind.

Today I'll concentrate only on The Stalwart. The Iron Lady. The Icon of Kinnygarden, Mrs. Case. She had a steely glare. Mrs. Case could pierce your very heart with a mere glance. This was bone chilling to a grade school upstart who was yet to kick the morning cow manure from his shoes. Everyone toed the line with Mrs. Case. She was the General.

Note that I am assuming that some of these teachers are long since dead. Either that or extraordinarily advanced in age. This way, I can comfortably write about them and not fear recriminations. I've already gotten my share of miserable grades. To be sure, though, I'll say nothing that is overly injurious to them. Especially Mrs. Case.

I know, I know, Kinnygarden. Who was it in my class that pronounced it that way?

I think it was Ed Bush. He always manufactured his own contractions. He was good at it, don't you think? Comes from the little kid propensity to talk too fast. Develops into a language of its own. But, hey, that was 55 years ago. We've all slowed down a bit since then. I, for one, can't talk nearly as fast as Ed could back then.

Our class had an unusual Kindergarten ritual each afternoon. The class took a nap; I guess this was Mrs. Case's answer to the ancient South American custom of siesta. As you might imagine, it was not usually an occasion for much sleep. Let's face it. We were five years old! Much more fun just to wink and giggle! Plus, we all lay on the rock hard floor, although, in fairness, the General did allow each of us to bring in our own blanket.

I still have my Kindergarten blanket, neatly tucked in a cupboard somewhere. I know what you're thinking: 'Small wonder it hasn't turned to dust by now!' I called it the Davy Crockett blanket. In some precincts across the land, an upstart Kindergartener would probably be suspended without parole for bringing that blanket to school. After all, it had multiple prints on it of Davy wielding a Kentucky rifle aimed at an Indian with a tomahawk. How politically incorrect is that?

Well, as fate would have it, on one particular day we had all stretched out on our blankets for the daily snooze. Initially at naptime, General Case would sit at her desk and shuffle papers until the class settled down. That would be her cue that it was okay to step out of the room momentarily to perhaps visit with a fellow teacher. So, we're all lying there unattended and nothing is happening, excepting perhaps a muted giggle. Suddenly a cock pheasant let out its distinctive crow, right outside the building. It was loud.

Everyone recognized the sound. Our area was densely populated with pheasants back then. Everyone knew how beautiful a cock bird was. A chance to get a close-up view of its plumage was too tempting. With the fellow so close to the windows, the entire class naturally bolted from the floor to sneak a peek. We were abuzz with our new visitor and he was beautiful. He continued to crow, each one more thrilling than the next.

Enter General Case. She was mortified! Her lips quivered with anger. She hadn't seen such insubordination since the Alamo. We all received a blistering tongue-lashing. It was ugly. We were not just out of line; we were reprehensible! The cock bird got away. We didn't.

Another day at the office, I suppose. I have poked a bit of fun here at Mrs. Case. I think her soul would forgive me. She was good for us. At the end of the day, we were sufficiently prepped for the rigors of first grade. Battle-hardened, you might say. If nothing else, we matriculated, one and all, to first grade.

FIRST GRADE - NOT ACCORDING TO PLAN

Hot dog, first grade. I made it! Kindergarten and Mrs. Case were behind me. This was going to be a cakewalk.

I caught the bus up at Kinkle's Corner. (It is now known locally as Connor's Corner.) The Kinkles, I guess, used to live in the house there on the corner. I never knew a Kinkle. I reckon they moved away before I arrived on the scene.

It was a mile walk from our house, so my brothers, sister and I had to hustle. Oh, I can hear it all now. You walked a mile to the school bus? Yeah, I did. And, you know what? We never missed the bus once. I will say this, though. I was not yet working much in the cow barn, so there wasn't any excuse to miss the bus.

There were two giant hemlock trees there at the bus stop. They made for a nice shady spot to catch the bus. They're gone now; have been for decades. They were taken down presumably because they were about half way into the road easement. Too bad. I loved those hemlocks.

Harold Wilson was the bus driver. In short order he got us to Alexandria Township School. It was there the class met Mrs. Leaman, one door down from last year's classroom. My classmates were all the same, except for Andy Chestikov. He didn't stay long with us, though. They were migrants, I guess.

Mrs. Leaman was a kindly, demure sort. She was no Mrs. Case. She was tall with grey hair, very slender, a soothing smile. She did her best. What else can one do teaching first graders? She was sort of a comfort teacher. With the exception of one incident, I don't recall a great deal of specifics about first grade. Perhaps a reality was setting in at that point. It was going to be one long slog before I got out of this place.

I don't mean to make it sound like a prison term, but I wasn't enjoying school to any huge degree. I began to contemplate my predicament along simple, logical lines. Let me see, I have eight years before I can move on from here. That's longer than I've been alive! Then, as I understood it, there were four more years of high school after that. To me, as a six year old, that seemed like an eternity. But, hey, I kept getting on that bus every day. If nothing else, Mrs. Leaman made it a bit more bearable than the previous year.

But, here I am, better than fifty years later, thinking about first grade. My take on the whole thing, even then, could have predicted things that happened decades later. Did I mention that I didn't really like school?

After my K through 12 slog, I went on to Rutgers. I didn't like that either. But the word on the street was that a college education was of paramount importance. So I went, but I quit after a year. It was the best thing I ever did. Studying Thucydides and the Western intellectual tradition wasn't cutting it for me. But, I digress.

Back to Mrs. Leaman. First grade was proceeding along as first grade should. Lessons were simple, the pace tolerable, even for those of a not-so-scholarly bent. One day, Mrs. Leaman gave us an assignment to work on at our desks and then did something rather quizzical. She walked to her desk in front of the room, sat down and rested her head on top of the desk as if to take a little nap. We expected her to be awakened by a few giggles, but that didn't happen. There she stayed, stock-still.

We wouldn't have known to call 911 even if 911 had existed. We just knew that this wasn't quite right. Fortunately another teacher happened by, saw through the glass in the classroom door and could tell that something was wrong with Mrs. Leaman. Within minutes, two other teachers were at Mrs. Leaman's desk, kneeling over her, whispering, trying to determine what was up. With one of the teachers on each shoulder, they lifted her and half dragged her out of the room.

Poor Mrs. Leaman tried to shuffle her feet as they assisted her from the room. She was crying as she left. Shortly Mr. Metzger, the new school principal, came back to the class and calmly explained that Mrs. Leaman wasn't feeling well and we'd be getting a new teacher for the rest of the day. The rest of the year was more like it; we never saw her again. In fact, she died later that day.

Yes, this was traumatic for us first graders. Witness the fact that I here recall it as though it was yesterday. At age six, you're just trying to grasp such a phenomenon. But Mrs. Leaman was gone. That was the reality of each following day until, like many resilient kids, we got over it. A string of substitute teachers ensued for the balance of the school year. Be that as it may, I will always remember Mrs. Leaman as our first grade teacher.

Come June, first grade ended. Who knew what lay in store next year? All I knew was that I was one step closer to the finish line and that it was summertime. A few months of pure delight lay ahead. Second grade would come soon enough. Next year's teacher? Who knew? That would have to wait, but it certainly wouldn't be Mrs. Leaman.

SECOND GRADE - SNAKE BAKED A HOECAKE!

Summer zoomed by. There had been plentiful adventure on the farm before the onset of second grade. Most memorable of those was with my buddy next door, Arlo Mitchell. We were the same age. We would play for hours in the woods. Hey, it was summertime and it was all good. Well, almost.

If you're OK for something a bit gross right now, find an illustration somewhere of the mouth of a lamprey eel. These are blood-sucking apodes that generally inhabit the Great Lakes. Their mouths are conic, with dozens of little fang-like teeth that allow them to fasten on to other fish and suck their blood. Now before you worry that I'm off on a totally incongruous tangent, hear me out.

Sandy Mitchell (he hadn't yet come by the nickname Arlo) and I were in the woods one day and we discovered maybe six or seven snake-looking creatures, four or so feet long, swimming in the near stream. What the heck were these? We'd never seen the likes of these creatures and we knew what normally swam in these waters. We stepped in the stream's edge, a move that would have scattered minnows in a hundred directions. These bad boys remained stationary. That was our cue to further investigate.

I bent down and put my hands closer to the water's surface, ready to pounce. They stood their ground. I grabbed two of them, one in each hand and yanked them out of the water. Wrong move. They writhed and twisted their long bodies around my arms strongly enough for me to know that I was in trouble. They wound more tightly and it started to hurt!

Arlo Mitchell to the rescue. He grabbed them, one at a time, and yanked at them hard enough that they lost their grip. Good thing I hadn't been out there alone. Arlo slung these fellows to the ground and killed each like a common barbarian.

I'd been rescued from what were, unbeknownst to us, lamprey eels.

What were these denizens of the Great Lakes doing in the streams of Tuckaway Farm? I blew it. This could have been my second grade thesis: Anguilliformes of Alexandria. Instead, we hiked our kills up to the barn where my father, being from Michigan, (as in Great Lakes) was incredulous. I never did figure out this biological conundrum. I was just glad to get the ugly things off my arms. It was a dramatic end to the summer.

The next week, second grade started. Our new teacher, Mrs. Frick, was a very genteel sort with a bouncy sense of humor; another 'comfort teacher.' But because she was fairly old and greying, how could an impressionable second grader not be reminded of last year's sad misfortune with Mrs. Leaman? Oh, well. No time for that.

The year progressed and all of us in the class gradually got the hang of it. Maybe this wasn't too bad, after all. Mrs. Frick helped in that regard. She had a flair for teaching little kids. She was almost making this stuff fun at times. In retrospect, it's my opinion that Mrs. Frick was the type of teacher that some parents pay thousands of dollars to find at a private school. Imagine that. Right here at Alexandria Township School.

Mrs. Frick would, at no apparent prompting, occasionally break into a little ditty that amused the whole class. I can still see her as she sang it to the class:
>Snake baked a hoecake.
>Set the frog to watch it.
>Frog fell a'dozin'.
>Lizard come and snook it.
>Bring back my hoecake!
>You long-tailed Nanneoh!

Was there some conclusion to be drawn from this? Hey, we were in second grade. Ours was not to necessarily draw conclusions. But, it was amusing and Mrs. Frick made it so. Sounded like something from Uncle Remus, but who will ever know?

* * *

Not long after that a bit of a controversy brewed at A.T.S. Mr. Duffy, the former principal, began to advocate for the teaching of foreign languages beginning in third grade. Well, if this wasn't a bit of cutting edge stuff. French and German in sleepy old Alexandria? It was more than most folks could handle. My parents fancied the idea but it never got past the school board. To this day I think it's a good idea, but then, how would modern day budgets allow?

If I may digress further, pondering this stuff prompts me to, indeed, draw some conclusions about my grade school education. Fifty years plus of perspective is beneficial here. No, A.T.S. was not a Blair Academy or some other 'prep' school that was the measure of a parent's wallet. But you know what? It didn't have to be. In retrospect, I would put up Mrs. Frick as an equal to any teacher that may have crossed our paths back then. She was very good at what she did. One might have asked, 'Ma'am, what are you doing here?' The fact is, there she was, and this was Alexandria Township School in the 1950s and 60s.

Hey, we all got our second grade education. We all, some more than others, were the better for it. That's the point, though. Every day, Mrs. Frick ran the same lessons by all of us. Seems like it then became a question of, what did everybody do with them? A.T.S. did its job. Did we then do ours? Years of perspective suggest the importance of what we chose to do with those lessons.

It seems fashionable for parents to challenge their local schools; and that's OK. A more worthwhile pursuit may be for them to challenge their kids. The world is full of educated derelicts. Is this the fault of schools? Undoubtedly, it is not the fault of Mrs. Frick, rest her soul.

At last second grade was over, one of my better years at A.T.S. It wouldn't be long before I would learn such nefarious skills as 'doctoring' report cards and the like. But, that's for another day. It was summertime and the lampreys had vanished from the streams.

THIRD GRADE, FOURTH GRADE - WHO'S COUNTING?

Third and fourth grade was the "black hole" in my grade school career. Why? Well, I am reminded of the movie *No Way Out*. My memory is a bit of a decrepit patchwork, but in third grade I was starting to wonder if there was any way out. There were ten more years to go, counting high school, and I was too young to even be thinking about college. To my third grade mind, this seemed endless. Life without parole.

But, it came time to start third grade. Enter Miss LaFalce. She was about 35 years old, the junior of any teacher that we'd had at Alexandria Township School. My perception at the time of what constituted a good-looking female was vague at best. About all I had glued together was that Miss LaFalce was quite young as opposed to prior teachers, who were quite old. There seemed a good chance she'd live out the whole year.

Was third grade a more enlightened school year than those prior? To be fair, I was starting a period of 'funk' in third and fourth grade. I wasn't engaged. I never learned those "times" tables. I suppose I was fraught with guilt over that one. I simply wasn't having that good a time.

More enlightened? I don't think so! Take, for example, our class trip that year. In first and second there had been a trip to Bowman's Tower, a trip to the Philadelphia Zoo. Those were fun trips. We may have even learned something.

In third grade we took a class trip to Milford. That's right, Milford, New Jersey. Some hack builder was in the middle of framing a few development houses. We saw studs in one. We saw insulation in two others. Oh, we got it. Walls don't just happen. But given the non-event that the trip was, I wonder to this day if maybe Miss LaFalce had something else other than studs going on with that hack builder. Ne'er shall we know.

Well, never mind. That's just my jaded third grade personality rearing its ugly head. But, it was an uninspired class trip, as was the rest of third grade. Fourth grade too, come to that. The boredom of school was starting to sink in. A.T.S. was losing me for a while.

Perhaps a child psychologist would have had a field day with me, but the closest thing we had to one of them was Mrs. Dinmore, the school nurse. I don't think she was analyzing many third grade psyches back then. Mr. Cole, the janitor, would have been better suited for that. I think he was more qualified.

* * *

Summer went by and fourth grade commenced. Enter Mrs. White.

I am reminded of an old buddy in college who we nicknamed 'Spare Parts.' His gait was very loose and angular. He seemed to gyrate as he walked, seeming like he might fall apart if he went much further. That was, of course, because he was put together with spare parts in the first place.

Mrs. White could just as easily have been nicknamed 'Spare Parts.' That, of course, didn't happen. As new fourth graders, we had not yet risen to the 'wise guy' level. Close, though, and I'm speaking only for myself. Surely Mrs. White bore the brunt before the year was done.

I can recall at least one or two memories from almost every grade at A.T.S., but details of fourth grade are sparse. Why, I'm not sure. I have no particularly negative memories of Mrs. White. She did her best. I can't even remember the class trip, but surely it had nothing to do with studs. No, not Mrs. White.

All of the rest of fourth grade is lost to me except for memories that are as ethereal as the distant sunset. What did I learn? I do recall that the bookwork was getting a little tougher. But, remember when Mom used to ask, "What did you learn in school today?" Were you ever able to answer that question for sure?

Presumably I picked up something. Mostly A's and B's were the order of the day; not to say that there weren't occasional slips a notch or two below. Doctoring those old, hand-written report cards became an art form. But, the stage was set for fifth grade. Hot dog! Progress was being made; there was light at the end of the tunnel.

Fifth grade would be the fulcrum point. Get through this and I'd be coming into the far turn. Make believe this was a horse race and it was bound to get more fun. Down the stretch I'd come. Who knew what lay in store? It was 1963. Summertime. Catfish are jumping and the cotton is high.

I have poked a little fun at my past teachers. That has all been in good fun. Be it recognized that theirs is a noble, yet under-appreciated profession.

I am most thankful for my elementary education, a la A.T.S. Kidding aside, my teachers did well by me. I regret that to express that sentiment to most of them, it would have to be posthumously.

FIFTH GRADE - COMING INTO THE FAR TURN

September 1963. Fifth Grade. This was getting better. In keeping with my imagined horse race, I was coming into the far turn. I was almost an upperclassman. A.T.S. was more engaging. Or, was it that I was more engaged with it? If I kept my nose to the grindstone, graduation was no longer in the altogether too distant future.

Enter Mrs. Yocum. A fifth grade boy probably couldn't have asked for a better teacher. For starters, she was cute. After all, this was still in the days of one teacher per grade, so whoever she was; you had to stare at her the day long. Lucky me.

I know what you are saying. "You were in fifth grade, Mr. Tucker. How much could you have known about cute?" Well, I knew enough to know that I was liking Mrs. Yocum, and that's all I needed to know. It didn't take a rocket scientist to figure it out.

She was probably a bit more than average female height, sandy brown hair, attractive face and build, quite good-natured with a real sense of humor. She maintained discipline, yet was subtly coquettish. How can I make such analyses from a fifth grade memory? You will have to take my word for it. I was paying attention.

Perhaps a few of those reading this are familiar with the inside of the building where my fifth grade follies took place. Mostly single story, linear; groupings of classrooms pieced together over the decades of occasional construction. Now Lester D. Wilson Elementary, the physical nature of the building symbolized in my mind the long slog that was grade school. Kindergarten started at one end of the school with annual advances to the other end. Eighth grade was a long way away.

Next year I would descend from my current classroom, down the stairs to the final row of three classrooms that face Schoolhouse Road. Call it the Home Stretch: sixth, seventh and eighth.

Mrs. Yocum would get me there.

(Not long ago, I had occasion to set foot back into my old kindergarten classroom. Mind you, I hadn't done that since 1959. Gasp! It was the closest thing I could imagine to a time machine. Vestiges of Mrs. Case. Holy Crow.)

It was mid-November. Fifth grade had been unfolding quite nicely so far. School was good. One day, quite unexpectedly, our school principal entered the classroom. It was rare to get a visit from Mr. Metzger, especially in the middle of a class. He usually wore a smile, but not today. He simply strode up to Mrs. Yocum's desk, whispered a few words in her ear and turned to address us.

He explained that he was delivering a message this afternoon to each class so that we all heard a consistent and accurate story before school let out. President Kennedy had been assassinated a few hours ago in Dallas, Texas.

Even to us fifth graders this was a grim message. The balance of the day in class was somber. I don't recall any tears, but our normally jovial class was sullen. This, of course, was not the first presidential assassination in America, but it was the first one in our lives, and last one that we wanted to live through.

Fifth grade. Age 10. Many of the awkward uncertainties of childhood, even in the earlier grades, had begun to dissipate. Perish forbid, a hint of maturity was showing in all of us. A hint, that is; no more than that. Not to suggest that we were a classroom full of adult fifth graders, but we occasionally showed a flash of confidence.

We were pretty lucky when you think about it. No drugs were filtering through our school, and little if any bullying. Leroy George and Eddy Hager did get in a rip-roaring fight one day on the steps outside the eighth grade classroom, but that wasn't a bullying thing. Mrs. Keck, an all but elderly teacher, had the misfortune of getting too close to that action. I'll refrain from noting where she was hit by a flying fist, but it had to hurt!

Otherwise, the most serious trouble you could get into was kicking a ball during recess over Schoolhouse Road and the barbed wire fence into Muldock's pasture. There was in that case no choice but to trespass and retrieve it. Yes, those were innocent times. The worst that may have happened was a torn shirt from the barbed wire.

Of course, there was the day that eighth-grader, John Shoudt, slid into third base out on the playground and pretty well busted himself up. An improvised ball field, third base was a rock: a solid piece of river stone. Fast forward to present day. Can you imagine the lawsuits?

I did get into a scuffle one day there on the playground with Kermit Weeast. (Did I just say something about maturity?) During the fray, one or the other of us fell on, and pancaked, my metal lunchbox. I knew better than to ask Mom for a new one, so I very meticulously hammered it back to its original form. It remained in service long after that.

Kermit and I still amuse ourselves about that incident now and then when we see each other. It seems typical of agricultural areas for some of the native sons, the farm kids, to stick around for generations. This, of course, is why the participants in the lunch box incident can still joke about it some fifty years later.

* * *

Fifth grade, largely thanks to Mrs. Yocum, was an enjoyable school year. She was able to maintain an intricate balance between levity and discipline. I always craved summer vacation from school but, for the first time, I found myself thinking that I would miss this. Mrs. Yocum, wherever you are, you did one helluva job!

* * *

Through my years at A.T.S., it would be safe to say that my routine was not typical compared to that of most of my classmates. I say most. A few were "bustin' hump" just as I was. But getting up at 4:30 every morning and working the farm for better than five hours (counting both ends of the school day) certainly added an extra dimension to school. I got through it, though. It might have even done me some good.

But for now, adios fifth grade. Time to head downstairs to sixth. Out of the far turn and into the stretch. In the meantime, summer beckoned.

SIXTH GRADE - DOWN THE HOME
STRETCH

Sixth grade. Hallelujah! I was an upperclassman, if only in my own mind. Hey, one had to conjure something. Besides, consider the math. I had two-thirds of this grade school slog behind me.

And speaking of math, I have heretofore not discussed any of my grade school studies. As it happened, I hated math with a passion. Science? O.K. Spelling and English? Excellent. Social Studies, O.K. Recess? I was very capable. But math? I rebelled; even zoned out on the multiplication tables. Never did learn 'em. Turns out, I didn't need to. The hexadecimal abacus was invented later that year.

My teacher? Miss Casazza (Italian, maybe?). A local lady, she had the unusual quality of having a younger brother who was a classmate of my older brother at Del-Val, Delaware Valley Regional High School. In other words, she was a young damsel. She, too, was a lot of fun, a good disciplinarian and good at what she was doing—even though, if I recall correctly, this was her first year of teaching.

Have you ever tried to picture yourself as a teacher? First day of your first year.

I'm not sure how I would have handled that, but I very well might have choked. Surely you would have to be quite prepared. What if you're not? Are you going to tell the whole class to take a nap while you get your head on straight? That would impress the Principal if he showed up. Let's face it, the pressure's on. On you!

Miss Casazza handled it with aplomb. Certainly our class, pack of soaring intellects that we were, didn't perceive any first day jitters. In fact, the school year seemed to go quickly, another sign that a capable teacher was making it fun. Time was flying, but what all happened that year?

Although I have progressed here to sixth grade, my trip down Memory Lane at A.T.S. is still hobbled by one factor: memory! Believe me, with 50 years between today and when it actually took place, some details have fallen through the cracks.

This would seem then to be a good point to break my pattern and skip straight to eighth grade. You'll soon learn why the stories of sixth and eighth are inextricably linked. I'll cover seventh grade later.

* * *

Had there been a school newspaper at the time, I like to think that I might have had a field day with the situation. Talk about under the radar; it seems that Miss Casazza made her way down the hallway a couple more times than we ever noticed. Two doors down the hallway was eighth grade.

The eighth grade teacher was Mr. Ontko. Or was it that Mr. Ontko found his way down the hallway in the other direction to Miss Casazza? Maybe it was both. Either way, they were soon betrothed.

Imagine that. A budding romance in our very midst, and we kids didn't have a clue. I suspect that was because we kids were clueless. Ya' think?

Mr. Ontko was a cool guy, from up around the Wilkes Barre area of Pennsylvania, I believe. That made for occasional fun with the way we respectively said things. Haymow, for example. I said haymow, rhyming it with cow. He said haymoe. Who was right? Well, who was the teacher?

Mr. O, as we called him, had played minor league baseball with the St. Louis Cardinals organization. For an eighth grade boy, this was impressive stuff! On occasion we'd be playing baseball out on the less-than-standard field when Mr. O would step in to make a point or two. We felt privileged. He knew baseball.

Sometimes Mr. O would run the bases. Man, could that guy fly. He was fast! I can still see him speeding from second to third. There wasn't anybody in our class who was going to catch Mr. O stealing third base, even though he was wearing a tie.

Thanks for those memories, Mr. O. You taught me, and years later you taught my kids. You had an influence. I was saddened when, a few years back, I heard of your passing.

Mr. Ontko's class had been a tad more challenging. By eighth grade, you pretty much knew what you were good at and what you were not. It must be a genetic thing; with math I mean.

* * *

I have a distant relative, an English "man of letters," Joseph Addison, who is buried in Westminster Abbey. Accomplished chap, he was. You'll find some of his works in the Harvard Classics. I bet he stunk at math, too. But, genes being genes, it became clear by eighth grade that my strength was not in multiplication tables. This is not to suggest that I could write like Cousin Joseph.

Along about half way through eighth grade, it started to sink in. Soon it would be peony time. An A.T.S. tradition, each year the graduation stage was lined with an impressive array of peonies. Graduation was always fragrant. After that, a whole new chapter of my school career would soon unfold. How would high school differ from A.T.S.?

I had consistently attended football and basketball games up there, had for years absorbed the Del-Val stories of my older siblings. The prospect of moving on was exciting. Eighth grade was the finale. I feel sorry for kids who, for one reason or another, get moved from school to school with no real link to ground them at their next location. I was fortunate. I was well grounded for Del-Val.

SEVENTH GRADE - CAN'T IS A SLUGGARD, TOO LAZY TO TRY!

Timeline: Year 1605.

Place: The New World.

Pocahontas, daughter of Chief Powhatan, belongs to a confederation of tribes whose homeland is in what is now Virginia. Pocahontas is fraught with worry over the prospect of an arranged marriage that she knows will not work.

Fast forward.

Timeline: Year 1966.

Place: Alexandria Township School, my seventh grade classroom.

I blew the dust off my abacus and learned that there are 361 years between those two timelines. Yet one thing is still steadfastly true: any illustration that was ever rendered of the legendary Pocahontas yields a remarkable likeness to my seventh grade teacher, Mrs. Berger!

Mrs. Berger was considerably older than Pocahontas was when Pocahontas was having her pre-nuptial worries, but their mutual physical features were, nonetheless, notable. Jet-black hair and fairly dark complexion, she wore an air of seriousness on her face as though a worried woman.

Seventh graders are sinister in their ways. Never to her face, but we called Mrs. Berger "Pocahontas." Kids will be kids, you know. We shared many a seventh grade guffaw at the expense of Mrs. Berger. But let the record reflect right here and now, she was dedicated to her profession. She made us all toe the line.

Mrs. Berger would tangentially philosophize in the middle of a class now and again and, in so doing, draw some heavy-duty moral conclusion. We sometimes wondered where that tendency came from. She was as interested in building our characters as anything else. She mostly bristled at any student's contention that they couldn't do something.

She related the story of the little, under-sized locomotive straining to pull its many boxcars up an incline. With each slower and slower puff of steam, the locomotive's similarly timed refrain was, "I can't. I can't. I can't." But the locomotive kept trying and, just as it appeared hopeless, it reached the top of the incline and started heading down. Its refrain changed to a very rapid "I think I can. I think I can. I think I can."

"You see kids," she bellowed, "'can't' is a Sluggard, too lazy to try."

Well, I guess the story stuck with me. Here I am relating it verbatim a lot of years later.

Is there a visual here that would provide a transition from what I have just described to something of a lighter note? Maybe Tommy Hager passing by seventh grade with another load of silage? C'mon class. Everybody wave to Tommy!

* * *

Do understand that this was seventh grade. You remember, "coming of age." Pheromones were flying! Hormones were humming! A couple of girls in the class were starting to look mighty fine. They, of course, shall remain nameless herein to protect their presumed innocence.

But, of course, school dances ensued; quite the opportunity to get a little snuggling in when a watching eye didn't glare. But it did. The chaperone at these dances was—you guessed it—Pocahontas! She was the Dance Gestapo, very strict about the distance to be maintained between slow-dancing bodies.

Indeed, the rule was six inches. That may seem a little too stringent, but it allowed for the co-efficient of the drag. If bodies became too close, they'd be compelled to maintain at least a three-inch gap. You can't make this stuff up.

I swear to God, she actually patrolled the dance floor with a ruler. That made it easily demonstrable to all parties involved whether or not dance protocol was being followed. Getting a bit too familiar with somebody? You could be staring down the wrong end of a ruler.

Does anyone remember the tune, "Cherish" by a band called The Association? That tune was all the rage in seventh grade. It was the ultimate snuggle song. Call in the ruler for that one. When "Cherish" was being played, Pocahontas held her ruler like it was a tomahawk! It might have been a mushy song, but to Pocahontas it was the beat of war drums.

Obviously I poke fun here, and indeed, some of Mrs. Berger's methods were over the top. In retrospect, however, there was an undeniable place for her. She taught many things, things other than science and math, other than social studies or English. Indeed, she taught discipline and character. She taught about overcoming adversity. She taught about attitude.

She taught about things that would seem to be more in the purview of parents. Was it appropriate for us seventh graders to be brought up to speed on these subjects? I think it was.

Was it appropriate that such lessons came from Mrs. Berger? I ask, if not from parents, then who? Perhaps from private school or military school? Heck! We got that from Alexandria Township School. No extra taxes. Thank you, Mrs. Berger! You were one of a kind, a good kind!

This, of course, gives rise to questions about curriculum, appropriateness of curriculum, etc. I'll let school boards, parents and teachers figure that stuff out. I suspect, though, that the void that Mrs. Berger was trying to fill still exists in seventh grade classrooms across America.

As all grades did, seventh grade ended before we knew it. Once again it was time to hunker down on the farm for the summer. Things were changing there, too.

ONWARD TO HIGH SCHOOL—THE DEL-VAL YEARS

Hallelujah! The cows were sold. Alexandria Township School was history. I entered Delaware Valley Regional High School with the feeling that I was making progress.

Alexandria school had been in the middle of a cornfield. So was Del-Val. Other than that, they differed. Who ever heard of different teachers for each course, in different rooms? This was radical. To be able to move around the building after each class was a diversion that allowed the day to proceed faster. Following every 42 (or was it 48?) minute class, there was a little mini-parade.

Those were a packed three minutes. First of all, everybody fussed in their lockers for a few seconds. We didn't have lockers at Alexandria. And then there was all this rapture going on. How much kissy-face could be achieved in three minutes? Surely there were those who were attempting to break the record. That hadn't been part of the play-by-play at Alexandria either.

It didn't take long for me to get oriented, though, and my days at Del-Val soon became routine. Football season was soon to start. I loved football, but I'd never played on a team. This was the first time in my life when playing on an organized team was not precluded by farm work. This was sweet.

There was not an abundance of players for Del-Val freshman football. If you had any interest in or ability at football, you played the entire game, offense, defense and special teams. I was a fullback on offense, an inside linebacker on defense, kicked off and was exhausted at the end of our games. We had a losing season but we had fun.

I was pretty badly injured during my sophomore year. Torn knee ligaments and torn cartilage put me in the Hunterdon Medical Center for an operation. Oddly enough, the doctor who performed that surgery committed suicide less than a week after the operation. Apparently, he felt badly about the job he'd done on my knee. It's OK, Doc. The knee has held up just fine.

My leg was in a full-length cast for a while. It was difficult working horses with that thing on. My knee healed eventually, but my football career was over. I spent the rest of the season and all games of the following years in the stands.

* * *

In high school, for the first time, I faced the grim possibility of failing a course. Weakness in anything to do with math was in the Tucker DNA. Maggie Carpenter was my freshman Algebra teacher. We seemed to have a mutual dislike of one another. I definitely had a serious dislike of Algebra. I passed, but by a margin so infinitesimally small, it took a mathematician to figure it.

JOY WAS MY WORLD

And speaking of rapture, in my freshman year I took a bus to a Del-Val basketball game and sat next to Joy Kutzman, a girl with whom I'd become friendly. She was in my class. I wasn't going to argue with the guys who opined that she was the best-looking girl in the whole school. By the time the bus ride was over, Joy and I were friendlier.

Joy had an affable personality. She was no soaring intellect, but what freshman guy cared about that? She already had a boyfriend, a hotheaded farm boy from Holland

Township. When he learned about that night's bus ride, he went on a bit of a rampage.

Without a hall pass, he angrily paced back and forth in front of the classroom door where he knew I would be. The whole school was abuzz, assured that a major brawl ensued. That never happened. Good thing. I was a lover, not a fighter. I managed to talk my way out of it.

Joy and I dated through all of high school and through all of college, most unusual for childhood sweethearts. But as time moved on we realized that we were quite different people. That didn't seem to matter so much in the earlier days. However, it seemed as though our relationship had painted itself into a corner. After nearly ten years we were still kids, but it seemed our destiny, almost an obligation to each other, to get married.

We did, but you can guess what happened. A couple of years later, we split. Our divorce was amicable. We see each other occasionally at class reunions. Our conversations are always positive. I would only extend a wish to any couple in the midst of a divorce that they might have one as peaceful as that one was.

It would be understatement to say that Joy and I gave it the old college try. I wish her only the best.

HIGH SCHOOL POLITICS

Was it ego? Was it sense of duty or service? Was it just the right thing to do? Whichever was the case, I became involved in student politics... about as involved as a high school kid could get. Class officers or student council members didn't accomplish much of significance, but they had a role. It was a laboratory. It was a significant part of my education in high school.

I ran for, and was elected, president of my class. I believe it was my sophomore year. What did I and my other class officers do? Actually, I'm having trouble remembering, but I am reasonably sure it wasn't business of profound, international consequence. We coordinated dances, fund-raisers and the like. Otherwise, the class of '71 was ably represented at Del-Val.

I also ran for and was elected to Del Val's Student Council. Student Council had further reach in that in that it was designed to mimic the organization of state government. Indeed, there was a NJ State Student Council that represented the collective voice of New Jersey students at the high school level.

Understandably, that voice attracted limited notice, but even so it was a time of serious unrest in New Jersey and nationally. The Vietnam War was full-bore and, yes, there were profound social issues in NJ. Our cities were racially divided. Many folks were food-challenged.

Del Val English teacher and Student Council advisor, Gretchen Waterbury, encouraged me to run for president of the state council. That would involve making a speech before a statewide gathering of student council representatives at the RAC, the Rutgers Athletic Center on College Avenue in New Brunswick. This country boy was something in a fish out of water.

I scrawled out some words on tablet paper, delivered them at the podium to a packed house at Rutgers and came to find out that I had a modicum of talent for public speaking. They seemed to like it. I was there elected president of the New Jersey State Student Council.

Over the next year, I gave several speeches having to do with the ugly divisiveness in the country. My role as a young kid calling for calm seemed to have appeal. One day I was scheduled to address the New Jersey Association of Secondary School Principals in Paramus. On the speaking roster that day, I was first. Next was New Jersey Governor, William Cahill.

My speech elicited robust applause. The Governor was introduced next. He first leaned on the podium and asked the audience, "Now how am I supposed to follow that?" It seemed I had done OK.

The next day, in the Bergen County Record, there read a headline, "Tucker Wows Educators."

I still have that clipping somewhere.

After that, Duke Carl, my junior history teacher, nicknamed me "Pontifical Pete."

TIME FOR CAP AND GOWN

High school came to an end; over before I knew it. The year? 1971. Yes, I was asked to speak at graduation. My address, entitled, "The Art of Compromise," was made in the same conciliatory tone that I was noted for.

When I was writing it, I recall words of disappointment about the subject from Ed Sampson, school librarian. I was yet to even think in such terms, but Ed was a more to the political left than I was. He wanted something a little more "firebrand" in my speech, something a bit angrier about what was going on in the country.

I told him I'd do what I wanted to. I didn't even realize it at the time, but this was my first introduction to the fact that American education professionals listed hard to the left.

Indeed, I was a little on the straight and narrow side of life. It's no wonder. I grew up in an agrarian setting. My parents were quite strict. I never even had a beer 'til I got to college. But boy, did I make up for lost time!

Forty-four years after I gave that speech, Jude and I were invited to dinner at the lovely home of Carlesse Kinney Ohlhaver in Bonita Springs, Florida. Carlesse and I had been classmates at Del-Val. To spark some lively conversation, she had put at my place setting a copy of the program for our graduation ceremony. (Who can still put their hands on that?)

"What was the title of your graduation speech that evening?" Carlesse thought for sure she had me over a barrel. I cogitated for a moment, then nailed it.

The power of recall is an amazing thing. I think Carlesse was amazed, too.

ON THE BANKS OF THE OLD RARITAN

Rutgers University accepted my application. I hadn't the faintest idea what I wanted to do when I grew up, so continuing my education seemed as good an idea as any until I figured it out. Truth be told, though, by the time I got to college I was sick of going to school. That's all I'd ever done. Did I really have to slog through four more years of this stuff?

Further, I had only enough savings for one years' worth of college. I wasn't making sufficient money to be able to cough up another three years' worth without burdening myself with student loan debt. I refused to do that. Something would have to give.

Despite my less than ideal attitude, "I settled down in this noisy college town on the banks of the old Raritan." How many times did I sing those lyrics at fraternity parties? Yes, I joined a fraternity, but only to put a roof over my head. There was a serious housing shortage at Rutgers.

Clare used to harp on the value of schooling. "You never waste an education," he would say. Exactly what did he mean by that, I wondered? Was he trying to justify the road that he had taken? Here was a guy who had studied at University of Michigan Law School, and he'd ended up milking cows. I know that people chided him about that.

In retrospect, I think Clare had a pretty sound philosophy on education. I believe what he was saying was, no matter what you do in life to put bread on your table, have a store of knowledge. One never knows when your knowledge about something will play to your advantage.

Well, enough philosophy, I thought at the time. That's all well and good, but I'm paying the freight here. I was fourth in the birth order. Any financial help that Mom and Dad could muster had long since been depleted. I was on my own, but that was OK by me. I had the freedom to handle this college thing the way I saw fit.

I had fun at Rutgers, but it wasn't really the life for me. I was anxious to get on with the business of making some money. My lack of funds was wearing thin. Not to mention, I wasn't thrilled with my courses. To boot, I found the political atmosphere at Rutgers to be repugnant. There wasn't much there to hold my interest. I finished one year, but except for a lame attempt at night school for a semester, I didn't go back. My school days came to a crumbling conclusion.

I am well aware that there will be grandkids and great-grandkids years hence who may be reading this. I would emphasize, kiddies, that what I have related to you here was my experience, only in the context of these memoirs. My experience does not mean that it should be your path to follow.

In the meantime, be aware that the world is full of educated derelicts. I employed a fellow for years who drove a truck for me, but I could never get him to improve his disheveled, unkempt appearance. His approach to his job wasn't much better. However, he was very well educated, far more so than I. That you have an education is much less important than the person that you have chosen to be.

Be your own best advocate. Follow not your whims, but your gut and, God willing, you'll get out of life what you want. Try to do what you love to do, even though whatever that is may not dawn on you immediately. Be patient, and do take notice: you become what you think about most of the time.

Whenever it is that your school days end, it does not mean that your education should end. Keep reading. Keep doing. Keep challenging yourself. Always learn.

BUDDIES

A RENEGADE FARM KID

Think of all the kids that you attended grade school with. A slew of them, right? For starters, there were all of the kids in your class or maybe a year older. Then there were kids two, three or four years older. Beyond that, there wasn't much getting to know them. Each year was an added age barrier. But, of all the kids that make up your grade school memories, is there one who absolutely stands out? One that is, hands down, the most compelling, funniest kid of the whole bunch?

For me, it was Tommy Hager. He was probably four years older than me. Barriers notwithstanding, we would exchange amicable acknowledgements of each other when passing in the hall. At first blush, one wouldn't think him to be an outrageous character. But he was! He would do whatever possible to annoy, terrorize, fluster, flabbergast and frustrate teachers and principal alike.

Tommy was about average height, maybe a tad shorter. He was very strong and stocky, and looked straight off the farm, as indeed he was. In fact, he lived and worked on the farm immediately adjacent to the schoolyard. At recess,

Tommy didn't play with the rest of us; instead, he pedaled his bike down the hill on Schoolhouse Road and up the other end to his house. But that was his recess.

Mechanically inclined as he was, Tommy had mounted a police siren to his bike. It was rigged so that the blare of the siren intensified as he pedaled faster. He would pull out of the schoolyard, get a full head of steam heading down the hill and let that thing rip about halfway down. One may have thought they were standing on Central Avenue in Newark! The playground would erupt with laughter. Suffice it to say, he loved the attention.

Some of my readers may find his name familiar. Yes, this was the Tommy Hager of Flemington stock car racing fame. For years, stock car racing at the old Flemington Fairgrounds was a mainstay of local entertainment. Tommy Hager was an icon at Flemington Speedway.

Once Tommy arrived at home while the rest of us were out playing, there'd be a lull on the playground. That's because it took a few minutes for Tommy to gear up for his next act. We knew what was coming. The view of Tommy's farm from the back of the schoolyard was perfect. We would all be lined up, dozens of us, like cattle penned in by the barbed wire fence. None of us was at all interested in playing catch or the like. We were waiting for Tommy Hager's next performance.

Behold! The Hager barn door opened. Out came Tommy's old jalopy, engine sputtering and missing noisily. He would gun the thing, pedal to the metal, full bore, wide open down the hill before a delighted student body. At hill's bottom, and top speed, Tommy would turn the jalopy 180 degrees and head back up the hill—that is, if he didn't flip the old battlewagon over in the process. We always expected that to happen, but he was a pretty good driver even then and never did flip it. In one recess period, there would be many repetitions. With each one, a roar erupted from us eager onlookers. This was pure entertainment, school kid style.

Occasionally the school principal, Mr. Metzger, would come out to the playground to see what was happening. He wasn't joining in the student's glee. His face was red with fury, but there was nothing he could do other than shake his head. His presence there served only to rev Tommy up a little more. Oh, well. What was a principal to do at A.T.S. in those heady days?

It was not unheard of for a farm kid to take a day or two off from school now and again to join family for a crop harvest. Tommy Hager certainly did that. Now, it takes a day or two of chopping corn to fill a silo. But here's the twist: much of the land they were harvesting fronted on Rte. 513. Of course, that's the same road on which A.T. S. is located.

So, every hour or so, Tommy would come chugging down the road on a big John Deere pulling a chuck wagon full of silage, and turn the corner at the school. The tractor was loud and very visible. He'd pass the sixth grade room, then the seventh and the eighth, all the while gallantly waving and smiling. He'd even stand on the tractor as though on a parade float. This, of course, riveted the attention of all kids in those rooms and totally disrupted any point that any teacher was trying to make. Again, there was nothing any of the teachers could do. Tommy loved it. We loved it.

One day Tommy brought a monkey to school. Where he got it, I never knew. But who cared? The plain simple fact was that a monkey was in the seventh grade classroom. A clever job he made of it, too! Apparently, as class began, no one was aware that monkey security had been breached in the first place. The teacher, facing the blackboard, turned around to face his class and was beset with kids laughing hysterically and a monkey scampering wildly about the room.

Now, how about a moment of empathy for the poor teacher? You know that if you were in his shoes, you'd be angry yet at the same time caught up in by the hilarity of the situation. But it was his job to re-gain control of the class, and determine culpability. Whose monkey was this, anyway?

Initially no one would fess up. There was only one piece of concrete evidence: the monkey. But, given past transgressions, suspicion eventually centered on Tommy Hager. His smirks only betrayed the obvious. His monkey gig was up! Tommy was given enough time to take his monkey back home and return to class. You've heard the expression, "The monkeys are running the zoo." On that day at A.T.S. they were for a while!

While putting this book together I thought it would be wonderful to have a phone conversation or maybe even a sit-down chat with Tommy. Surely that would add immeasurably to my vague recollections. And besides, I hadn't seen the guy since our school days together. If anything, he might be pleased to know that his grade school antics were going to be immortalized, to some small extent.

So, I went online to find Tommy. A few days went by, then a short matter-of-fact reply came from an auto racing association. Tommy Hager passed away a few years ago. This burst my bubble. Most of the folks that I've been writing about lately I know are long-since departed, but Tommy? We were in A.T.S. together. Tommy, it seems just yesterday that I watched you roll by the school window with yet another load of silage.

Time is going too fast, old buddy. Bless your soul. Rest in peace. And Tommy... thank you.

GROUND HIVES

As kids, Arlo Mitchell and I spent as much time as we possibly could getting to know every square inch of the old Hartley farm. How lucky were we to have a hundred-plus acre playground? We got to know it pretty well.

We were scrounging around down in the woods one day when Arlo had the sad misfortune of kicking up a hive of bees. He managed to really piss them off. They swarmed all over him before he even knew what was happening, and they started to sting him! Again and again and again!

A helpless feeling it was. Arlo swatted with a fury... again and again. I tried to move him away from the swarm, but it was hopeless! The bees knew their target. We were fortunate to be close to a stream, so I started slathering his whole body with cold mud. Arlo was one hurtin' cowboy.

We made it up to his house, a painful trudge. His Mom drenched him in the shower and surveyed the damage. Poor Arlo had been stung 42 times! He hung tough. Surely he smarted for the next couple of days.

I have since punted a few hornet's nests myself. It's never fun, but Arlo's 42-sting record has never yet been broken.

ARLO SAWS THE FIDDLE

A distant but familiar sound would regularly emanate from the Mitchells' house. It was a series of hideous, disjointed screeches: my buddy, Sandy "Arlo" Mitchell, was learning to play the violin. The Mitchells were a family of accomplished musicians. I loved to listen to Mrs. Mitchell play the piano when I was a kid.

Arlo slowly but surely progressed. As time went by he became really good. In later years he cut a few albums, one of which is part of my all-time favorite listening repertoire.

Fast-forward many decades. Arlo is playing with an Irish folk band, The Shenanigans, at Tommy Makem's club on 57th Street in Manhattan. Jude and I went in to see the show. Indeed, there was a distinct Irish flair to the crowd. Hootin' and hollerin' was going on!

The band switched gears for a minute as Arlo embraced the microphone. With fiddle at the ready, he said, "This one goes out to my friend in the audience tonight, Pete Tucker from Pittstown, New Jersey!"

With that, Arlo and the band launched into that very notable Bluegrass tune, "Orange Blossom Special." They played it with a vengeance; Arlo's fiddle at warp speed! The crowd went nuts! They loved it; right there in the middle of

Manhattan. Bluegrass fanatic that I am, I was ecstatic. Resounding applause from the audience ensued.

I couldn't help but savor this unlikely juxtaposition. There we were, Arlo and me, two country boys, buddies since age two who used to play in the sandbox together, enjoying this spectacular moment in the middle of the greatest city in the world. Life was good.

GOOD MORNING VIETNAM

I have already mentioned the name, Wally Knight. He was probably eight or nine years older than me. He was thus highly revered in my mind; a guy that I looked up to and admired immeasurably. He was buds with my older brother, Dan.

It's a wonder that Wally even made it to Vietnam, because he had plenty of opportunity to get himself killed well prior to that war. He did things on horseback that defied all good common sense. If there are any horseback riders in my audience at the moment, you might well agree.

How's this for a mounting technique? Stand on the ground, maybe twenty feet behind your horse. Line yourself up directly facing the horse's rump. Get a fast running start. Using your momentum when you have reached the rump, stretch out your arms, place hands just above the tail and catapult yourself up into the saddle. Voila! I watched Wally do it lots of times.

There was one other complication. Wally's horse, Minxie, was only so patient with this routine. In fact, at the split second of Wally's landing in the saddle, Minxie would let go with a tremulous kick of both hind legs. Not that Wally ever gave it a thought, but what would have happened if Minxie made a split-second anticipation of the landing?

That's right. Lights out, Wally Knight!

* * *

In the early days of the Vietnam War, Wally was there, as an infantryman. I never had opportunity to talk with him upon his return from Nam, but brother Dan went hunting with him afterwards. Wally was apparently wired a little tight from the war. Hitting the ground when a distant shotgun fired may have seemed to be an overreaction, but Dan hadn't fought in the jungle. Wally had.

Dan, though, had since sailed with a Merchant Marine company who shall here remain nameless. While his ship was docked in Saigon, Dan was "borrowed" by a certain government authority (again not to be named), because of his ability to "read a river." In this case, the Saigon River. The object was to avoid running ships aground, especially without any knowledge of what the cargo was. This was wartime.

Another unsung hero of my immediate childhood was, again, probably nine years my senior. Joe Milligan's folks, Emmy and Bert, were solid and righteous folks, mainstay members of our church, Bethlehem Presbyterian. Their dairy farm was adjacent to the church grounds.

Did Joe enlist or was he drafted? I'm unsure, but he wound up an Air Force fighter pilot in Vietnam. In 1967, his plane was shot down. All the Air Force could tell his aggrieved parents was that Joe was seen ejecting. The war dragged on, and five years later there was still no word about his fate. Emmy and Bert aged noticeably. Their son could be in a Viet Cong POW camp or maybe dead. Who knew?

Then, in 1973, Hanoi announced that it would soon release video footage of some POWs. This was big news, a first in the war where progress toward peace seemed forever stalled. The much-watched Huntley-Brinkley newscast of NBC was to air the video that night. At supper, Mom, Dad, Dave and I gathered around the tube, fraught with anticipation.

Unbelievably, the first face that we were able to make out was that of a very gaunt-looking Captain Joseph E. Milligan. We all screamed ecstatically. Mom immediately phoned Emmy, who had been glued to the same telecast. Her relief was Heaven-sent!

The delight of any childhood Christmas morning paled in comparison to this occasion. Joe Milligan was coming home. A priceless gift had been given.

Joe's subsequent account of survival as a POW, when I read it, was riveting, something no man or woman should ever have to experience. After tributes, medals for valor, and an honorable discharge, Joe returned to his farming roots. He studied and became a veterinarian, practicing somewhere down South. The last time I saw him was in church when I was in eighth grade.

Five years after that, I lay in my dorm at Rutgers listening to the radio call out numbers that dictated one's status in the military draft. I lucked out by a wide margin. Viet Nam was not to be in my future. Had I been called, of course I would have gone, although I had mixed feelings about our being there. Politically, Vietnam was a far cry from The Necessary War that Dad and his brother fought in.

Even though I had more than a bit of guilt, knowing what my earlier contemporaries had been through, I was nonetheless happy to have dodged the Vietnam bullet.

THE CLINTON TRIANGLE

The name was coined by Majchrzak and Yost, my two best buddies at Rutgers. It was prompted by an inexplicable series of fairly dramatic weather events that, over a period of time, took place whenever they paid visits to Tuckaway. The phenomenon became so consistent that these fellows became wary whenever their travels brought them near the Clinton area. A visit to Tuckaway became synonymous with the dreaded "Clinton Triangle."

The first episode seemed innocent enough. Doing some chores, the three of us had loaded up my pick-up truck with bales of straw to take over to another location. We were driving out Tuckaway lane when suddenly a ferocious wind blew up. This was no ordinary breeze; it was very forceful. It was cyclonic. That's right, tornado-like.

Where the heck did this come from, all of a sudden? A funnel of leaves swirled 25 feet in the air. Branches twisted out of treetops. A cedar tree was wrenched out of the ground and hurled into the air. There I was, driving my truck right through a mini- tornado!

I was bewildered. Yost and Majchrzak were incredulous, but it was over before we knew it. We had to stop before we reached the end of the lane. A tree had been dropped across it. We sat there for a moment in stunned silence, realizing that we had just dodged a bullet. None of us had any idea that this was going to happen.

We turned the truck around and headed back down the lane to get a chainsaw or two. We'd have to saw our way out to the road if we wanted to continue our errand. Turns out, there was considerable cleanup to do from this episode. It had been no ordinary weather event. Indeed, Yost and Majchrzak had just had their first brush with The Clinton Triangle.

There were other freak weather conditions when my two college buddies visited Tuckaway over the years, which added to the notion that something was awry. Rather than drawing any rash conclusions, I am resigned to attributing the whole thing to circumstance. Majchrzak and Yost may not agree with me. And in any event, it's more entertaining to perpetuate the notion of the Clinton Triangle.

JOHN FINN, WE HARDLY KNEW YA

It was getting near college time for Dave. I, of course, was two years behind him, but we were both full-bore in money-earning mode for college. We sought house-painting jobs. That was a far better bet than most teenage employment.

One day we were painting a house located off of Rt. 579, not far from Tuckaway. The house was set back into the woods a little, nicely located. The owners were never at home when we were on this job. Because of where we sat to have lunch this day, we noticed a narrow path that led into the woods. Curiously, we'd been on the job a few days and hadn't spotted it.

With owners away, we resolved to extend the usual half hour lunch break to explore the path a bit. It was a lovely day for a stroll, anyway. The path was lovely too, though a bit overgrown and in need of a machete. We continued with no particular expectation of finding anything and, indeed, we just got further into the woods. We'd never been here before. This may have been a hunter's trail.

About to turn back, our curiosity implored us to venture one more turn. In so doing, we made a strange discovery. Among tall weeds and gnarled brush stood a small, single story house. Almost storybook in its appearance, the house itself did not at first seem abandoned.

There were no broken windows or other signs of vandalism, minus the effects of bygone winters. However, it soon became obvious that no one had been in residence for quite some time. That, of course, was from the outside, looking in! There was a story here. What on earth was it?

Well, we'd come this far; what harm to look into the windows?

We did, but they were so dirty that we could barely glimpse anything inside. We could make out some furniture, but that was all the windows would allow. At this point we figured, why not walk around the house to check if a window was somewhere left unlocked? Before that, let's just make sure that the front door windows don't allow any visibility.

I grabbed the door handle just to steady myself at wiping the glass. To my surprise, it turned all the way, and swung open.

Ah, the unseemly notion of breaking and entering. We were hardly burglars, but curiosity had smitten these cats. What was the harm in a quick house tour? In we went.

Surreal doesn't begin to describe it. It appeared as though someone had just neatened up, walked out of this house and never came back. How long ago, who knew? A bed was made. The table was neatly set for dinner, including salt and peppershakers.

A telephone sat on a side table. For the hell of it, I picked up the receiver. There was a dial tone! This was getting creepy. A neatly arranged group of magazines lay on the same table, complete with the glued address label. They read: John Finn, Hampton, New Jersey

Even so, there was little in the way of answers. Where are you now, John Finn? Have you ever been back here? Are you still alive? Who is the table set for?

We had to get back to work before some ghostly visage closed the door behind us. We returned to the job leaving everything at John Finn's exactly as it was. We'd be back, sometime.

Fast-forward a couple years. I introduced my Rutgers roommates to Tuckaway. We got a little buggered up that night. Two city kids, I thought I'd test their mettle a bit. With a little flashlight, we ventured to John Finn's.

I soon found out that my roommates, Majchrzak and Yost, were scared out of their wits. They weren't too accustomed to being this far into the woods. I had shared with them my account of discovering the place two years back. They already had the heebie jeebies and we hadn't even reached the house yet.

When we did, from what our little flashlight would reveal, things appeared to be exactly the same. However, in the dark, the place was more eerie than I remembered. Nothing had moved. The table was still set; the phone still had a dial tone. How could that be? Wouldn't service have long been shut off by now?

Then, without even a warning flicker, our flashlight lost power! There we were in John Finn's house completely in the dark. Through the window, there was a wee sliver of a moon that alternately appeared between the clouds. My guests were becoming a little unsure of themselves.

As though further creepy effects were needed, a screech owl started tuning up deeper in the woods. Majchrzak and Yost had reached their limit. It was an eerie sound that they'd never heard before.

"Hey, Tuck," Majchrzak said. "Let's get out of here!" That was fine with me.

We groped for the door, stepped back outside and bolted.

Forty-four years later, the three of us still occasionally reconvene at Tuckaway. Now and again we'll invoke the specter of John Finn's house, but we've never gone back.

I wonder what we'd find if we did?

IN MEMORIAM

Jim Kennedy was a classmate of mine. We were buds. His mom happened to be a secretary in Del-Val's office. She was very well liked by the students, by the staff, by everyone. Jim's younger brother had just entered Del-Val.

Then, tragedy. The three of them were heading up Riegel Ridge Hill one day. His mom was driving. A truck heading down the opposite side of the road was hauling a Low Boy construction trailer. Somehow the thing became detached, veered into the oncoming lane, and struck the Kennedys' car. All three were killed instantly.

The next day at school, there was stunned silence. All day long, a dropped pin could have been heard in the halls. How could this have happened? High school had taught us one of life's cruelest lessons, entirely outside the curriculum. Disbelief was punctuated only by sobs.

To this day, whenever I drive by the little Catholic Church in Milford, I am reminded of the saddest funeral that ever was. Jim Kennedy, his mom and brother were gone.

Jim's dad, a staunch Del-Val supporter and also extremely well liked, was, needless to say, devastated. By the grace of God, Jim's two older sisters were there to help him move on in life.

LOCAL COLOR

PARTY PHONE LINES

My, how telephony has changed since the time when our number was 195-R11. I'm too young to recall the days when, upon making a call, you picked up the receiver and said to the operator, "Wilma, get me Harold." However, at Tuckaway we certainly had party lines.

For those not in the know, these were not phone networks for teenagers to discuss upcoming parties. Party lines simply meant that the phone in your house was on the same circuit as that of one or two of your neighbors. If you wanted to make a call and Paul Fritsche happened to be on his phone, you had to wait 'til he was finished.

That's just the way it was. Paul and Chris Fritsche, the Mitchells and the Tuckers were all on a party line, and all could hear each other's conversations if they were impolite enough to listen.

Juxtapose this scenario with the budding, pre-teen romantic interludes of the Mitchell girls. These required protracted chats on the phone. Sometimes those conversations would hit seemingly interminable, awkward lulls when neither speaker knew what next to say.

The next aspiring user of the phone line would pick up the receiver, sense from the tone that it was busy and yet hear no conversation. So, the expectant user would linger on the line for a moment. Still no conversation. It became something of a Mexican standoff.

Eventually, improvements were made and everyone's house was on its own circuit. Developing romances could progress with telephonic ease.

MAKIN' MOONSHINE

Dad needed a tool that he didn't own. Our near neighbor, dairyman Paul Fritsche, would probably have what Dad needed. Dad trekked up to Paul's barn, seeking to borrow. When he arrived, Paul wasn't there. His brother, Bill, was milking. Bill didn't normally milk. Something was up.

Upon inquiring, Bill informed Dad that Paul was in jail! Turns out, unbeknownst to everybody, Paul and a few other local fellows had been running a still in a remote building at nearby Camp Marudy (now Camp Tecumseh, run by the Salvation Army). The place was a stone's throw from the Fritsche farm, and good-sized, a tad under 400 acres.

This was not the usual start to anyone's day. Dad shared a few moments of levity with Bill, borrowed what he'd come for, and took the tool home. He then promptly visited the jail. Like a good neighbor, he posted bail for Paul Fritsche and the day got back on an even keel.

Apparently, some on-the-ball law enforcement guy had noticed that someone out in Nowheresville was using huge amounts of sugar—truckloads, in fact. And there was also a lot of hooch coming from somewhere out there, which meant an illegal still was in operation. So it was a fairly simple matter to follow a dump truck load of sugar heading from the Newark area out into the remote regions of Hunterdon County.

The truck led the cops right to Camp Marudy, where the whole operation got busted. Now, some fifty-plus years later, the story is no more than an old story of Alexandria lore. I have only one regret. Being much too young at the time, I never got to sample any of the stuff!

WEEKLY LESSON IN HUMILITY

Lewald Harvey and Reading Gephardt each wore jodhpurs when they came to the farm on weekends. That's right: jodhpurs. They looked ridiculously out of place. This was a down and dirty dairy farm, for crying out loud! We wore Wrangler jeans and work boots caked with cow manure.

To raise a little extra scratch, Clare boarded two horses for these gentlemen. They came to ride most weekends... in their jodhpurs. Tuckaway was, and still is, a beautiful place to ride. Gephardt and Harvey took full advantage of that, but there was a rub with these two.

They were amiable enough chaps with reasonably pleasant dispositions. Gephardt was a lawyer in Clinton. Harvey, I believe, owned a local insurance business. Clare gave them a sweet deal. Each horse had a run-in stall, all the hay it could eat, and Dave and I cleaned their stalls each week. For all this Gephardt and Harvey each paid Clare $35 a month.

But wait: there was an added bonus. If these gentlemen of the gentry would simply call the house ten minutes in advance, their horses would be brought in from the pasture and latched in their stalls, such that they would be immediately ready for bridle and bit upon their owner's arrival.

I didn't fully grasp that ours was a service business as it related to Harvey and Gephardt. I only knew one thing: when Dave and I wanted to ride, we had to catch our own horses. Gephardt and Harvey stunk at catching their horses. We watched them try once. Their mounts kept running away. They needed us to do it for them, every week.

It was an exercise in humility, having to catch their horses. I had to wonder, if I wore jodhpurs, who would prepare my mount?

A.D. MACAULEY

Albert Darby Macauley was a frequent visitor to Tuckaway and a colorful character. He wasn't just being sociable. He bred cows. More precisely, he was an artificial insemination technician for the Northeastern Breeders Association.

This wasn't your typical, ho-hum job. A.D., as we called him, travelled from farm to farm all day long with a tank of selected, frozen bull semen, and serviced dairy cows that were ready in their cycle to be bred.

Already, the story gets unsavory. Preparing for his dirty deed, A.D. would pull on a long, rubbery glove reaching the full length of his hand and arm. Then, as you may have guessed, A.D. would slide that gloved arm straight up the cow's rectum to manipulate her ovaries and sundry parts, preparing them to better receive the semen.

Exactly what he was doing up there, I'm not sure. Obviously he was working blind, but he must have known what he was after. At times, he would extract his arm, express dissatisfaction with the way things were feeling, and re-enter. Of course, A.D.' s job was easier if the cow didn't kick. You might further understand why the cow would want to!

One day A.D. came to the farm to service a cow and had forgotten his glove. In fact, it was in the afternoon and he'd been working since morning. He'd been working gloveless all day. It was incumbent upon me to inquire if that didn't bother him.

"Only when I pick my nose," he said with a smirk.

OLD FOES MADE GREAT FRIENDS

Heinz and Annalise Bluemel lived over in the beautiful Hampden area of Franklin Township. Socially, they got on in grand style with Mom and Dad. The Bluemels had two kids in the same age range as my siblings and me.

Occasionally our family would go over to their house for dinner, the evening would grow long in the tooth and all us kids would fall asleep. That would last only so long because the adult folks would get into the grog a bit and their guffaws would soon awaken us. The same thing would repeat a few weeks later when the Bluemels dined at the Tuckers'.

This association was heartening in a few ways, not the least of which was the fact that in earlier years Dad and Mr. Bluemel had rather different backgrounds. Both men had served in WWII, but in starkly different ways. Clare Tucker, as you already know, served on the USS *Massachusetts*, a battleship. Heinz Bluemel, on the other hand, was a pilot... in the Luftwaffe, Hitler's Air Force.

As kids, we were mildly aware of this difference. It didn't really matter to us much, I think because it didn't seem to matter too much to Heinz Bluemel and Clare Tucker. But even as a kid, I had to hand it to both men. Certainly they knew of their curious situation. Certainly they were aware of the gravity of the conflict in which they'd taken part. Surely, they were aware that when they came home, they were among the fortunate; they had survived.

What was impressive to me was the way that the two men were able to put it all behind them, forget former woes and proceed in life as good friends. Further, that Mr. Bluemel emigrated from his native Germany, learned English and succeeded in business as an electrician here in America. I'm sure that his past allegiances must not have worked in his favor at times.

Heinz and Annalise are probably no longer with us. If they are, they're very old. Their kids? We've lost touch, so I have no idea. Writing these words is yet another reminder of how tenuous old alliances become with the passage of time.

A WILY WOODSMAN

None of us expected a knock at the door that night. It had already been dark for a couple of hours. We hadn't heard any car come down the lane, nor seen any headlights. No dogs had barked. No sound of a truck splashing in the potholes. Yet there it was, a faint rapping at the front door.

No cause for alarm, though. Alexandria was pretty innocent country back then. It was just unusual, that's all. With a slight hesitation, sister Sue got up and opened the door a crack. Nothing but darkness.

"Hello," Sue said. No answer. She opened the door a little more. "Hello?" Again, no answer.

Sue put her face a bit closer to the opening. Something was there. It took a few seconds for her to realize that she was staring, from a few inches away, at the business end of a single-barrel shotgun.

"Just wanted to ask if I could go 'coon huntin'!" Sue's shoulders slumped in relief. It was a familiar voice.

"Darn you, Paul Cochran! You scared the daylights outta me!" Sue exhaled. "Dad! Is it OK if Paul Cochran goes 'coon huntin'?"

"Tell him to come on in and say hello," Dad called.

Shenanigans along this line were standard procedure with Paul. Yes, he loved to pull practical jokes and laugh, but surely the gun wasn't loaded. Paul stepped in the house, leaned his shotgun on the wall and launched into small talk with Dad.

Who saw what buck on whose farm, whose combine was broke down, how many pigs he'd killed today for Charlie Em. Of course, the stall cock on Tucker's F-20 Farm-All he still needed to replace.

This was Paul Cochran's world. There weren't many immediately significant things. He was a mechanic, a butcher, a farmer; whatever he did, he did well. And, truth be told, Paul did a lot of other things. He was a neighborhood go-to guy.

Short and burly, with a more than ample beard, Paul looked like someone out of an ancient photo you might see in a tattered album of foot soldiers dating back to the day before the battle of Chancellorsville. His visage was alive and vibrant. Just listening to his day-to-day descriptions of things was pure entertainment.

Paul knew a lot of things about a lot of stuff. From time to time we put beef in the freezer, not an Angus or a Hereford, just some milk cow that produced poorly. A Holstein fattens up like any beef breed anyway. Paul would do the slaughtering and butchering for us. The "kill floor" as I called it many years later in my abattoir days, was the center bay of our machine shed. Crude set-up, yes. Not U.S.D.A. inspected.

An overhead beam allowed us to rig a pulley to hoist the carcass, allowing for evisceration, skinning and hanging. The trusty F-20 provided the muscle to lift it up high enough. Surely you've heard the expression, "there's more than one way to skin a cow." Indeed, there is. What did we do with the offal? Well, buzzards have to eat, too.

Mrs. Mitchell, Sandy's mom next door, didn't seem to care for her kids to watch the slaughter in process at our place. Why not, we would wonder. This was lively entertainment. As far as we kids were concerned, this was the only place on the farm to be at that particular moment.

Of course, there was no refrigeration in our "slaughterhouse," so the process had to coincide with sufficiently cool weather. A nasty cold snap was something you didn't want. Butchering a frozen solid beef carcass isn't fun.

After ten days or two weeks of aging it was time to do the butchering. Paul would do the primal cuts and we would carry them up to the basement where the wooden egg-candling table became Paul's butcher block. As a kid, I enjoyed this part, not that I ever really learned the difference between a porterhouse and a chuck steak. It was a confined space where I could listen to the conversation between Mom, the meat wrapper, and Paul Cochran, the butcher. Highly informative stuff it was.

Time passed by. I grew up and learned a few things. I don't know if the homeland butchering experience had anything to do with it, but years later I learned that trade from A to Z. I think that had more to do with having to put a roof over my head, but somehow I think Paul Cochran might have been pleased. The more I learned in life, the more I gained respect for a guy like Paul. To know as much as he knew took a lifetime's worth of experience.

Paul's house was well up on a wooded drift way off of Woolf Road. It was the measure of the man and I quite enjoyed visiting there. He obviously was a busy man. All you had to do was look around his place. Parts from an engine job he was doing, a baler knotter, a pile of split wood... various and sundry items that I knew nothing about. Paul was putting fixes on a bunch of things.

So, what became of Alexandria's consummate 'coon hunter? Sad to say, Paul Cochran has long since passed on. But he remains indelibly etched on my mind, a man who enriched my childhood immensely. I can't help but hope that my few words here do him justice. At times we wonder what we'd say to someone like Paul if we hooked back up in the afterlife. I think I'd just say, "Thanks, Paul. Could you take me 'coon huntin' with you just one more time?"

Jude's first visit to Tuckaway, July 1979.

Teaching Heidi to drive at Tuckaway, May 1991.

Union Township, Hunterdon County. Jude and me looking to get a little taut in the traces! July 1987.

Haying at Tuckaway the old-fashioned way. I stack, Jason drives and Jude heaves. Circa 1986.

Our wedding day at Bethlehem Presbyterian Church, Grandin, N.J. From left, Flower Girls Sunshine & Vanessa, Bridesmaid Trish Porreca, the happy couple, Best Man Jason, Ushers Martin Gransky and Charlie Mann. July 25, 1982.

Final bale from the Big Field. Yours truly on the Allis Chalmers, Jason with the bale, Sunshine calling it a day! June 1989 at Tuckaway.

Sesame Place in Pennsylvania, Our kids and their cousins, from left: Sunshine Thomas, Jason Thomas, Krista Tucker, Vanessa Thomas, Danielle Tucker and Jennifer Tucker. Summer 1982.

"The Baker Field" at Tuckaway. Now, why would I rake hay in a white shirt and tie? Simple! Hay needed raking during office hours! June, 1993.

Sunshine's Wedding Day, about to head to the church. Tuckaway, Nov. 4, 2000.

The family off the Columbia Trail, High Bridge, NJ, 1984.

My neighbors used to call me The Woodmonger. I never understood that! Tuckaway, November 1996.

Eating the profits! For years, Dad ran a pick-your-own strawberry operation. Here, Vanessa and cousin, Krista Tucke put a hurting on the day's bottom line. Tuckaway, June 1983.

Jude and I on a blissful day over in Union Township. You see, I did get off the farm once in while! Summer 1988.

From bottom, Vanessa, Jennifer Tucker, Danielle Tucker, Sunshine, Jason. Tuckaway Bradford, August 1989.

Little Heidi, born on the farm in May 1988, still one of Judy's go-to saddlehorses at the time of this publication.

WORK AND FAMILY LIFE

THE STEED BREED

Having left college, I bounced around for a while. My first business venture, in combo with brother Dave, was with Steed Industries Inc. Steed had a location in Paramus, N.J. They marketed a decidedly superior petrochemical product, an engine additive competing with the commonly known STP. It was a very good product.

Problem was, Steed operated under a multi-level marketing system. Turns out Steed was far more interested in selling distributorships than in selling product. They were eventually indicted for fraud. The whole company fell apart.

Interestingly, there were many other investors in this scheme with a whole lot more smarts than Dave and I put together, but we all lost our investment. Lesson learned. As the 1927 poem "Desiderata" stated, "The world is full of deceit and trickery." Was he selling Steed, too?

After the Steed debacle, I lingered in the Paramus area for a while. I got a job as a construction laborer, then another as a roofer. I'd become the quintessential college dropout. I was homesick; missed Hunterdon County, missed Tuckaway. But I figured that I simply needed to be patient and something would turn up.

I answered an ad for a butcher's apprenticeship and got a job at a Foodtown supermarket in Bergen County. I had to join a union to get the job. No choice. How fair was that, I wondered in my naiveté.

I was eager to learn the trade. I went on lunch break and returned in 15 minutes to get back to work. No, no, no, barked the shop steward. Taking less time than required for lunch was against the rules. This was my first lesson in trade union mentality. Do only what you have to do. My work ethic had been shaped on the farm. That ethic flew in the face of Local 464, Amalgamated Meat Cutters!

BACK TO HUNTERDON COUNTY

I moved back to Tuckaway, then rented a little ramshackle house in Franklin Township so I could live by myself. A LaneCo supermarket in Clinton snatched me up right away for their meat department. This wasn't glorious work or superior pay, but I had already learned the virtue of learning a trade. Consistent employment was mine if I wanted it.

However, there were some unsavory characters at that particular store. I didn't realize how poorly two of them got along. They shall remain nameless, but one of them came back from lunch one day, brandished his pistol there on the cutting room floor and emptied it into his co-worker. This incident appreciably depleted our staff. One was totally disabled; the other was in jail.

I got to know a fellow named John Person. He had a custom butchering and slaughter business in Stanton, servicing local farmers who raised their own beef for their own freezers. He needed help. After I'd worked with John for a while, he proposed that we set up a partnership. Person and Tucker Meat

Processors was born of that conversation. Our working relationship was excellent but after a year or so, I started having second thoughts.

This was brutal work. Was I going to be doing this five or fifteen years from now? I felt badly, bowing out of my arrangement with John, but I did what I had to do. I loved John. We had lots of fun working together. He was most understanding but, bottom line; he was dealing with an unsettled kid.

(Special note: John Person passed away a few months prior to my writing this. RIP, good buddy, and thank you.)

BUTCHER'S BUNGLES

An incident or two that occurred during my stint with John Person are worthy of note. One day we were tearing apart the butchering facility in a defunct Acme supermarket in Flemington. We had hefted an exceptionally heavy freezer onto John's pick-up truck, and were hauling it to our facility in Stanton. That required that we drive a couple of miles on Rt. 31, one of the area's busiest thoroughfares.

The freezer was too long to allow closing the truck's tailgate. We would have to proceed slowly. So there we were, sitting at the traffic light in front of Hunterdon Central High School. The light turned green.

Now, any other two halfway intelligent guys should have scoped out this situation, but we did not. From hauling many hindquarters and forequarters of beef, the bed of the truck was smeared with slippery beef fat. John needed only slight acceleration to slide that freezer off the truck and smack in the middle of Rt. 31. Oh, brother.

John immediately pulled the truck off to the shoulder, so it was not quickly obvious to the passing drivers why a freezer was in the road. Talk about rubbernecking! We just stood there and surveyed this debacle. In need of a little comic relief, I observed to John, "This is another fine mess you've gotten us into, Stanley."

Well, we had manhandled this behemoth onto the truck, so surely we could get it off the road. A couple of other motorists were kind enough to stop to help. Four of us were easily able to start inching the thing toward the roadside. The greatest complication to that effort was bumper-to-bumper traffic.

But, the gods were merciful. We moved the freezer off Rt. 31 before we were blessed with any police presence. I was unsure what we were going to say had that happened, maybe something about fighting the Cold War!

* * *

Another time, an Angus steer hurdled a corral panel in the slaughterhouse holding pen one day, an amazing feat. This spelled trouble. One doesn't re-capture an Angus by holding a grain bucket under its nose, especially if it already senses what is coming. In no time it had sprinted a half mile from the slaughterhouse.

Henry Bundt's farm wasn't far away. John and I knew two pertinent things. One, Henry had a tractor with a front-end loader, and two, he also owned a 30-06 high-powered rifle. Shortly, Henry was in his tractor's driver seat while I sat on the fender with the rifle. This steer was coming back without the dead-or-alive option!

After a cautious approach, I asked Henry to let me take the critter down. I knew exactly where I wanted to hit it. Thankfully the rifle had a scope. We were about as close to the steer as we were going to get; in other words, not very close.

BANG! A perfect shot. We approached, chained its hind legs to the loader and hoisted it up. I drew my knife from my scabbard, stuck the steer and let it bleed out while Henry drove back to the "house."

Getting a steer all riled up like that before the dirty deed doesn't auger well for tenderness of the meat, but we'd done what we had to do. This was a well-finished Angus, anyway. It would be fine in anybody's freezer.

When we returned to the slaughterhouse the USDA inspector simply shook his head. What would he see next? He was certain that his wife wouldn't believe this one!

(A special note is in order here. I had no sooner finished writing the above words when I read in the paper that Henry Bundt had passed away. Was that more than coincidence? RIP to a wonderful gentleman.)

* * *

I had already moved on from the butchering business and landed a job selling real estate. Some would say that instead of slaughtering cows, I was now slaughtering people. I maintained a pretty close friendship with the Persons. John's son, Johnny Bell, or JB, stayed in touch. We had often worked together. At the end of a day at my new job I was perched at the Clinton House bar, having a tonic and gin. Louie, the bartender, answered the phone behind the bar and handed it to me.

It was JB. He needed help for a peculiar adventure. JB had just received a call from Steve Perchaylo, a Kingwood Township dairy farmer who we'd done work for in the past. Steve was in a fix. His big Holstein bull had just busted loose in his barn and was wreaking havoc with his whole milking herd.

The bull had gotten so frenetic, as Holstein bulls will, that Steve had to drop it right there in the feed alley of his dairy barn. Drop it with the help of a bullet, that is. Could we come pick it up, take it to the slaughterhouse, dress it out and make a pile of hamburger?

OK, readers, Meat Processing 101: the only thing that you can do with bull meat is make hamburger. No steaks, no roasts. Bull meat is way too tough. That bull would have to have been castrated long ago—made a steer—for the beef to have any quality whatsoever.

Next, we asked Steve if he had bled out the critter. If he didn't do that soon, the blood would coagulate, rendering the carcass not viable for anything. Steve said he'd try. We said we would be there as quickly as we could.

Easier said than done. Person's pick up wasn't immediately available. I had to go home, get out of my three piece, pin-striped suit, change into real work clothes and wait for JB to pick me up, whereupon we had a seven-mile drive to get to Perchaylo's. If this all came together in enough time, it would be a miracle.

When JB and I finally arrived at Steve's place, we surveyed the situation and found that, indeed, we were too late.

"He's already set up," I told Steve, evoking a concrete metaphor. Despite his attempt to bleed out the beast, most of its blood was already coagulated. The bull carcass was worthless.

Well, what to do? Since we were already there, and as an act of good customer service, JB offered to haul the carcass back to the slaughterhouse and have the dead stock service company come to pick it up. Steve was appreciative. With his front-end loader, he hoisted the huge carcass onto JB's pick-up. The bull was so big that it barely fit. In fact, its head and neck drooped over one side of the truck body.

You might imagine what that looked like to the oncoming driver as we drove back. We did get some double-takes. We were, also, getting hungry. There was now no hurry to get our useless cargo anywhere, so we opted to pull into Dunkin Donuts in Flemington for coffee and a jelly-filled.

An innocent-looking teenage girl was working at the counter. The only available parking spot was right by the front window. When we pulled up, she rubbed her eyes and stared in disbelief. Perhaps that was because the bull's tongue was hanging out, I wasn't sure.

JB and I exited the truck and headed to the entrance. Our little damsel looked panic-stricken, almost as though the bull had stood up, jumped off the truck and was following us into the store.

I would love to have heard her description of this to Mom, upon her arrival back home later that night. Surely Mom would have suspected drugs!

THINGS START TO LOOK UP

I sold real estate for a while. At that time, Jim Weichert hadn't been at the business for too long. He opened his fourth office in Clinton. This was circa 1976. I worked in that office for a while, well before Weichert became a national real estate juggernaut.

Things were coming together for me. I didn't have any money saved yet but I had the opportunity to buy a house, a tiny little bungalow nicely located contiguous to Tuckaway. I had always liked the place, even when I was little, but how was I ever going to pull off the purchase of it? Whoever said that where there's a will, there's a way?

Getting the 80% mortgage was the easy part. To complete the balance of this 100% financed transaction, Jim Weichert arranged with Chatham Trust Co. to loan me the rest. This was the first of two huge breaks to befall me in a short period of time. This transaction was the beginnings of my farm. The other was the beginning of the rest of my life, marrying Judy and, by extension, my family.

Just across the street from the Weichert office was a storied dining establishment, the Clinton House. One waitress in particular, Judy Thomas, I had occasionally seen strutting across the street on her way to work. She was hands-down good looking. I decided I would have to make my way over there for a casual cocktail.

I was still married at the time, but that was hanging on by a thread. Judy, I learned via conversation with her, was not only married but had three kids. So much for Judy. Nonetheless, I would occasionally drop in at the Clinton House if for no other reason than it was a watering hole just across the street.

I still wanted to spend a little more time with this lady. What could I do to cajole her? On a blistering hot summer day I left a note on her car there at the Clinton House. I wrote that watching her stride into work was like sitting poolside on a scorching hot day and not being able to jump in. Turns out, she appreciated the metaphor.

In a subsequent conversation with Judy, I learned that we had simultaneous divorces going on. Oh, the timing! Now I just had to convince her that I was her knight in shining armor. Later, a visit with her at my little bungalow in the woods seemed to help in persuading her. But wait a minute. What was I doing? Was I just going to get out of the frying pan of marriage and into the fire of a rebound relationship?

Judy had similar reservations. We didn't communicate for a few months. Then along came St. Patrick's Day. I called Judy on a whim and asked her to meet me down at the Pittstown Inn for a few green beers. I'm glad that I made that call. The rest is history. Thirty-five years later as I write these memoirs, Judy sits in the chair beside me.

Getting to know Judy was a blast. The kids were precious, but they didn't come with an instruction manual. Was I crazy? Was I going to marry this woman and inherit three little kids all at once? That hadn't been in my playbook, but I loved Judy. I also loved Jason, Vanessa and Sunshine. I figured I'd better fasten my seatbelt. This was going to be my long haul.

When we were married, I was a bit crestfallen when, given their choice, the kids opted not to take on their Mom's new name. Was our family going to be perpetually divided with two names? Jude and I with one, the kids with the other, their biological father's name. Would that be divisive? Awkward?

Turns out, it was wearisome explaining it over the years, but I had to remember this was the kids' name when they were little. It would be awkward for them to change, too. We all came to live with it.

Raising the kids was not only a growing experience for them. It was for me, too. In retrospect, I feel for the single parent. It's a tough enough job for two. Judy had been doing it alone for a while, yet what a task it was for the both of us. How Herculean it would have been for one.

As it turned out, we raised some good kids. They all did well in school and got good college degrees. Good jobs.

Certainly bettering their parents, none got divorces. So, it seems we did something right. Who needs to read those instructions anyway? Are there things that we would have done differently? Of course. Welcome to parenting.

BUILDING A HOUSE - BUILDING A FARM

When I first met Jude, she and the kids lived in an orange house. I'll never forget my reconnaissance mission, following her directions to see where she lived. You see, even in the countryside there are good areas and not-so-good areas. Jude and her soon-to-be ex lived in the not-so-good area of Franklin Township.

Her house was built of ceramic blocks that were, yes, orange. Neither Jude nor her then-husband made copious amounts of money, so it was all they could afford, but even so... orange? Right from the get-go, Jude and I made jokes about the color. I suggested that we give the property an exalted title: Orange Place. The name stuck.

Regarding co-parenting, I was not in my comfort zone. The understanding here was that I would become father to children who called someone else Dad. That someone else I did not particularly care for, but he came to visit my kids-to-be most weekends. This was far from comfortable but this arrangement had uncomfortable written all over it from the outset. Obviously it wasn't the kids' fault.

As I contemplate this, so many years later, it is so abundantly clear that I should never have allowed this insignificant discomfort to enter my thoughts. Who was it, many years later, that Vanessa asked to walk her down the aisle in her wedding ceremony? Sunshine as well? It was me, highly honored. The family had developed in remarkable fashion.

But, now back to the Orange Place timeline. What would Judy and I do next?

Well, I suggested, let's move the whole shebang to my little house in the woods. Jude and I discussed it, and decided to move. We'd set ourselves up for a mountain of work, but we were happy. The kids adjusted.

My new era at Tuckaway had begun. My Mom and Dad had sub-divided the land and sold their house and 15 surrounding acres. This, of course, was the house in which my siblings and I had grown up. Mom and Dad moved to Bradford County, PA. Incredulously, they thought that the area around Tuckaway had become too "built up." They retained ownership of 46-plus acres of the old farmstead and moved north to colder country. More on that later.

Jude and I had two big tasks when we moved to my house, which, remember, was contiguous to the farmstead. First, we had to make the house much bigger. As it was, things were going to be very tight.

Second, Mom and Dad would eventually want to sell the rest of the land. Wouldn't it be sweet to attach our three acres to the remaining land and buy it from them? It was a very tall order, but if Tuckaway was going to remain nearly intact, that's what we would have to do. Farm boys don't give up easily on the old homestead. It's in our DNA.

Our first addition to the house was a master bedroom. The original house had one bathroom, a living room and kitchen, and two bedrooms. But now, with three kids, that was a bit cozy. Over the years, as our wallets would allow, we made four more additions to the house. A big challenge was to not make it appear piecemeal. This is why God created architects.

During this time, more contiguous land became available. The next-door Baker farm was being sold. The broker sliced it up a bit to effect a sale. We were able to pick up twelve extra acres that we merged with Tuckaway.

We eventually made a deal with Mom and Dad for the remaining land of Tuckaway. Dad made a point not to "give" it to us. To his credit, he wouldn't show favoritism to any of his kids. Market price would be his price. But, after all of these mergers, acquisitions and additions, Tuckaway was finally back to its original size in terms of acreage; and our house was much bigger than the old original.

How many years did all of this take? Too many, but we finally had home glued together the way we wanted. Although we borrowed money to get it done, it was essentially a pay-as-you-go proposition. As I write in 2016, the farm has long since been paid for.

TESTING HER METTLE

I was aware that the Beekeeper's Trail hadn't had any maintenance for a long time. In the days when Jude and I were just getting together, it barely warranted the title of "trail." Ragged Edge Path would have been more like it. To this day, I'm not aware of any specifics as to how it became known as the Beekeeper's Trail. I can take a guess, though.

Maintaining beehives in this neck of the woods is nothing new. Farmers have done it to pollinate crops for many decades, not to mention to sweeten their gruel. I can only assume, then, that some predecessor of mine kept beehives around this farm and as far away as a man could walk. In so doing, his shoes trod a path between the now Tucker Lane and the more obscure Brandywine Trail. In maintaining his network of hives, he, by default, created the Beekeeper's Trail.

I'll bet that is as good a guess as anybody will come up with, this surely being the way that lore is woven. At least it brings us back to the subject at hand. I was fixing to take Jude on a horseback ride. Where would we ride? Making our way to the Brandywine would make for a fine ride through beautiful country.

I inquired as to her riding experience. Jude assured me that she had ridden before. She seemed confident. I was aware that sometimes people engage in bluster about their ability to horseback ride, about some distant lesson that they received on a merry-go-round one time, but that wasn't my read this time.

So, we saddled up. Sure enough, she seemed capable in the saddle.

We rode north on Tucker Lane to the point where we made the turn to intercept the Beekeeper's. A gnarled mess it was! Russian Olive, Multi-Floral Rose and other insidious vegetation combined to thwart our progress. It was slow going to the Brandywine. Jude's blouse got torn in a spot or two, her glasses were knocked off and any semblance of a good-hair day was out of the question.

So far, the ride was telling me volumes about the lady of my interest. This, I soon realized, was an episode that many women would have turned into a drama. I, myself, was getting beat up by this ride. I started to feel guilty. Why hadn't I taken the time to check this trail before I took her up here? Too late now. We were both challenged, but Jude was keeping her sense of humor. Make no mistake; this was not enjoyable riding, but Jude was still making light of it. Hey I really liked this lady!

We finally made it to the Brandywine Trail. We reined to a stop for a breather whereupon I uttered two words that she has never let me forget. "You passed!" As though she was being graded. The nerve of some guys.

There sat this fine lady, her saddle stuck with thorns and twigs, her blouse ripped and her face scratched and I can only muster a snide little comment about her passing grade. Was chivalry all but gone? She had done a masterful job at braving the thicket. I only hope that, somehow on that day, I passed that sentiment along to her.

Nonetheless we had a great ride that day. I was quite impressed with her good character and we took with us a memory that we have revisited many times.

THE HO CHI MIM TRAIL

Mim was a nickname that our son Jason fabricated for his mom when he was quite young. In the meantime, and as an item of common jest, I would somehow try to incorporate Jude's name into naming specific locations around the farm. Thus, when I endeavored to blaze a trail around the total circumference of Tuckaway it was dubbed the Ho Chi Mim Trail.

As you may know, the Ho Chi Minh Trail was a frequently referenced enemy road system during the Vietnam War. Not to aggrandize the old Communist leader, the play on words was there, so I took it. The Ho Chi Mim, not Minh, remains one of my proudest accomplishments at Tuckaway. I blazed it for the most part by hand with cutting tools: a pickaxe and a beleaguered Homelite chain saw.

Why did I do this? It was an indulgence. What's that you say? Hacking through thicket and thorn, rooting through briar and brush was an indulgence?

OK, it doesn't take much to entertain me, but why bother to have this land without being able to traverse it, to enjoy it? Over the years, Jude and I have ridden this trail on horseback a thousand times if we've ridden it once. We have enjoyed the "Ho Chi" immeasurably.

Aside from this, the trail now adds to my vicarious life. As I write this, I haven't been on horseback for three or four years, due to health issues. I miss riding but seeing Jude and others ride still gives me great pleasure.

The "Ho" has long been a commonly used trail by local equestrians. How could I not take pleasure in knowing that the fruits of my toil are being enjoyed? It is not unusual in the course of a day to have more visitors via horseback than by car. I like that.

TREEHOUSE TRYST - FIVE GIRLS, ALL MISSING

The girls were age thirteen. That should have been enough for an Amber Alert right there! Vanessa and Sunshine had plans for the night. They and their cousins, Jennifer and Danielle Tucker, were going to sleep overnight at their other cousin's place. Krista Tucker had a nicely appointed tree house over at Krista's mom's house, not far from Tuckaway.

Their intent, or so they said, was to snooze through the midnight hours in Krista's tree house. Ah, the best laid plans! Actually, that wasn't their plan at all. Vanessa had amorous notions toward a schoolmate, Justin Cooper. Justin happened to be the County Prosecutor's son. They lived close by. Of course, the intent for all five of them was to walk to a previously arranged location to meet up with Justin and some of his friends.

There a pleasant little interlude would be had by all. Perhaps Krista's mom didn't have her guard up sufficiently when all girls departed for the tree house, make up and mascara so nicely applied. Tree dwellers are not normally such fastidious groomers.

Unbeknownst to the girls, Jane, Krista's mom, did the motherly thing around midnight and stepped out to the tree house to check on the girls and found the place deserted. This, of course, prompted some shouts into the pitch-black woods. After several attempts, a very concerned Jane phoned our house. Then Jude phoned Pat Tucker, Jennifer and Danielle's mom. I held down the fort while Jude drove over to Jane's house. It was going to be a long night.

The three mothers scouted the immediate surrounds, flashlights in hand, yelling at the top of their lungs. No answer. Concern grew. What had become of five teenage girls in the middle of the night, in the middle of the countryside? This wasn't good! Jane, Jude and Pat resolved to call the police.

The police came with some high-powered searchlights. The radius of their search expanded. They were looking for clues, footprints or, dare I say, bodies. The police searched for hours. Jude called to update me. It was grim. No trace of the girls had been found.

Jane's home fronted on Baker Road, outside of Pittstown. Along about 4AM, Jane and Jude heard laughter in the far distance. It drew closer and soon became discernible as girls' laughter. It was coming from Baker Road. The three moms ran to the mouth of the long lane. Merrily skipping down Baker Road were the five girls. The moms weren't sure whether to hug them or scream at them. They hugged them.

I had to get to work early the next morning, but agreed to step into the girls' room to give them a talkin' to before I left. Of course, the girls were deeply asleep. I woke them, and made them sit up and listen up. I talked to them about the dangers of what they had done last night.

They were barely able to keep their eyes open. Just as I was telling them that they were grounded for the rest of the summer, they appeared to simultaneously nod back off. I'd obviously struck the fear of God into them.

Our girls were safe and sound back home. That is what really mattered. Jude and I both went to work. Surely this wouldn't happen again. I never found out whether Prosecutor Cooper ever learned of his son's involvement in that evening's episode. If he did, he wouldn't have been too pleased.

POINT YOUR SKIS DOWN THE HILL

Stories about the kids would be nowhere near complete without tales of ski trips. And those tales wouldn't be complete without discussing my good friend, Charlie Mann. That's because my family was inextricably linked to Charlie over years of ski excursions.

Charlie grew up on the outskirts of Little York. Of course, Little York is outskirts to begin with. We knew each other as kids; we went to the same high school but we didn't really become tight until well after that. We would ski together as much as possible. Charlie looked so effortless going down the hill, it was just fun to watch him. I was sort of a hack on skis, but I could get down the hill. When it came time for my kids to ski, I taught them what I could. That instruction essentially boiled down to "just point your skis down the hill and go!" Beyond that, they got lessons.

One day on Bromley Mountain in Vermont, while the kids and Jude were all still pretty much green at skiing, we were ascending on the chair lift. I sat one chair behind them. The inevitable moment came at the top of the hill for all to spring from their chairs and depart from the lift. In so doing, Jude fell. Not only did she fall, but her bindings released her skis from her boots. The same thing happened to Jason and Sunshine.

Now, anyone who has skied knows the peril of having to depart your chair when, ten feet in front of you on the very ground that you must ski over, a yard sale is in progress. Randomly strewn skis, ski poles, ski boots attached to bodies are all lying there.

I managed to curve sharply around this muddled mass, realizing at the same time that Vanessa had not gotten out of her chair and would thus be heading back down the hill. Not a propitious moment.

It is incidents such as this that prompt the ski lift operators to stop the progression of the chairs, enabling the ne'r -do-wells to glue it back together for a moment. I never anticipated that my crew would precipitate such an episode, but they did. Presently, however, we sorted ourselves out and proceeded down the hill.

Jude's skiing ability was, well, improving. I recall times when we were skiing with Charlie. Understand that when Charlie and I skied together, we got down the hill rapidly! Jude would try to keep pace, but inevitably she'd fall behind. This was no problem at all. Charlie and I would simply pull up along the trail somewhere, take a breather and wait for Jude.

It appeared as though Jude was having trouble coming to grips with the fact that we men skied faster than she did. When Jude finally caught up, she would do her best to spray a dramatic cloud of powder all over our skis and say, "Keep moving, you jerks!"

This was almost as though Charlie and I had been skiing full bore all the while and Jude had just whizzed past us. We were more than happy to humor her.

* * *

Jude, the kids, Charlie and I took a lot of ski trips together. We skied at many places in Colorado: Vail, Breckenridge, Aspen, Steamboat, to name a few. We skied in Park City, Utah and Taos, New Mexico. On one trip, we made the long haul to Idaho. Charlie was driving with a lead foot. It was some distance from the airport to Sun Valley.

We had admonished Charlie about his use of the F-word around the kids. Things were proceeding smoothly with lots of giggles in the car. Do know that Charlie is one of the funniest guys ever. Then, suddenly, flashing police lights appeared behind us!

"Ah, f—k," Charlie blurted out! Well, the kids must have thought that this was the funniest thing they'd ever heard. The back seat erupted with laughter.

We enjoyed numerous ski vacations, including lunch at the ski lodge and the pounding down of many a beer. Now before you take exception to that notion, consider that many a skier swears by the practice of getting a little "tuned up" at lunch prior to resumption of the day's skiing. Some swear that such relaxation improves their skiing.

I won't comment one way or the other. After all, the grandkids may be reading.

BRACE YOURSELF FOR THE HAHNENKAMM

Kitzbuhel, Austria is a gorgeous place to ski. For the avid skier, the European Alps offer abundant challenge. I decided to accept that challenge one day and try to "smoke" the Hahnenkamm. Don't be deceived by its paltry 5627 feet in elevation. The Hahnenkamm, German for "rooster's comb" is a famed course on the World Cup ski circuit. It's no "bunny slope." On that day, it so happened that the most challenging portion of the course was roped off. They could have fooled me! I just wanted to get down the thing without having a yard sale. I managed to do that, but at the bottom of the Hahnenkamm, I was thoroughly winded.

At that point in my life, I had skied many a daunting hill. I didn't realize it at the time, but my skiing was being challenged by my MS. I am just glad of one thing. Before this disease started to mess with me too much, I got to ski the Hahnenkamm. Lucky me!

WHEW, THEY GREW FAST!

Where did the time go? What should I have done differently, or better? With the kids, it was over and before I knew it, they'd flown the coop. I got started late, so I had to hit the ground running. Thank God that Jude and I raised the kids together. I can't imagine doing it alone. I know people who have, or do now. They are heroes in my view.

Raising kids who are not your progeny means that you have skipped some of the early chapters in the process. Don't think that it doesn't leave a hole in your heart. It does! But, indeed, they become your kids. My kids. Our kids, and the hole is thus repaired. Thanks be to God. It takes time. It takes love, but a beautiful family was born.

Where to begin with the stories? They are too numerous. To only pick a few slights the many. Suffice it to say that it was a wonderful journey. Now, with six grandkids, it continues to be. How blessed we are. How blessed we have been.

The kids were given the experience of life on the farm; not the experience that I had, but that is just as well. They learned about responsibility. They learned about the virtue in performing tasks that weren't always their first choice. They learned about exercising their God- given ability to think.

I gave young Jason the task of digging a line of post holes, maybe ten of them. I laid out the line with a taught string and, with a shovel, dug the beginning of each hole, every eight feet. The holes had to be hand-dug, each three feet deep. It was a dead-straight line.

At the end of the day we reviewed his work. Indeed, Jason dug ten holes, each three feet deep. He had worked hard, but one of the ten holes was obviously askew. When I inquired about his deviation, he had no plausible reason. He did not disagree that this one hole was well out of the straight line.

Jason's work was not finished. To his chagrin, I instructed him to backfill the one errant hole and dig another hole in the proper spot. He did.

Jason learned a lesson that day: a mistake isn't really a mistake unless it's not fixed.

* * *

Sunshine didn't take kindly to collecting eggs. She went to the chicken house one morning and took longer than usual. She perhaps had a Mexican standoff with the cantankerous rooster. When she came back to the house, she was not amused.

The pockets of her hooded sweatshirt were bursting with eggs, meaning that she'd forgotten her egg basket. To add insult to injury, Jude thought this to be cute enough to photograph. Sunshine's image was thus captured that morning in a highly agitated state.

One Christmas morning Jude got the hare-brained idea to put bows on the sheep. Why I failed to talk her out of that notion escapes me. So there I went, kids in tow, up to the pasture. This was similar to a drill in football practice for open-field tackling.

The ground was wet, very wet. The kids and I did our very best to corner the wooly speedsters and wrestle them into a prone position. We all took a header or two in the muddy morass, much to the delight of the instigator.

We got bows on the sheep, but did it fill us all with Christmas cheer? One clue: we never did this again.

MY CAREER TAKES HOLD

Brother Dave and his first wife, Jane, had a little business. It wasn't a new idea; listings of upcoming television programming wrapped around local ads, printed on newsprint quarterfold. Nothing fancy. It was produced on a web press that couldn't trim worth a darn, but they were busy.

When Dave asked me to come work with him, I could see the potential, so I came on board. I sold ads; I laid out ads. Not having any experience, I learned as I went. The little rag grew. It evolved into a sort of quasi-newspaper that we called Today In Hunterdon. We published it for many years.

Jane eventually left the business. Dave and I drew up a Buy-Sell agreement between ourselves. We relocated from Clinton to Flemington and built offices in warehouse space behind storefronts in the Flemington Department Store parking lot. Tucker Publishing Co. was painted on the door in the alley for about twenty years; low cost accommodations, but it suited us well.

It so happened that Flemington, NJ was one of the first locations in the entire country where clothing, tableware and fashion manufacturers congregated with "factory outlet" stores. Every day, hundreds of tourist-shoppers embarked from busses to scour the stores in Flemington. This was a huge opportunity; someone simply needed to recognize it. The Tucker boys did, and we were already in the publishing business.

Most of these shoppers were from central or north Jersey, and were only vaguely aware of what stores were there or exactly how to get to them. Someone should put a map in their hands as soon as they got off the bus. That map should be in a magazine that included ads of the various stores. This "point of purchase" advertising should be produced by Tucker Publishing.

It was simple, but that was the beauty of it. We started publishing Shopping In Flemington. It was fabulously successful for fifteen years or so. It offered three key business qualities that any entrepreneur would want: low cost, recurring revenue, and scalability.

It was not as though I wrote a college thesis on this endeavor. As has already been noted, I had eschewed college after only a year. This business idea came clear to me simply by thinking about it.

The first quality, low cost, could be achieved by eliminating one of the primary costs of any print publication: distribution. Copies of Shopping In Flemington, or SIF, were free. Distribution was accomplished when shoppers voluntarily picked up a copy from our racks. Our only task was to keep filling the racks. By contrast, Today In Hunterdon is circulated by mail, a major cost.

The second quality, recurring revenue, was accomplished by the simple fact that we published SIF monthly. To sweeten the deal, most advertisers simply ran the same ad in each issue. Place that in the low cost column, as the production of ads was minimal.

The third quality, scalability, was the sweet one. These outlet store complexes began to crop up in many places. In Kittery, Maine, for example. So why not publish the Kittery Outlet Shopper? We did. In Orlando, Florida. Why not publish the Orlando Outlet Shopper? We did.

By the time the enterprise reached its pinnacle, we had ten such publications in print along the East Coast.

Business evolves, however. Dollar volume in these publications started to wane after years of a great run. My health issues weren't helping either. It seemed a good time to retire. Jude helped me search the Internet for a business broker. Dave wasn't ready to retire. I was, and the business was not trending well.

In early 2003 we sold Tucker Publishing to a businessman in Knoxville. The ride was over.

Knowing that someday grandkids will be reading these words, what nuggets from my business experience might I impart? What to do, what not to do?

For starters, not everyone is cut out to run their own business. It's not something that you have to do. Go with your gut, but remember that an employer will tend to pay you just enough to keep you from quitting. You will have to determine if that is acceptable to you.

Then, try to determine what it is that you would most enjoy doing. Let's face it: going to work every day to labor at something you dislike will not make for a grand career. I wasn't really successful in that regard. I didn't particularly like the publishing business. I gleaned enough enjoyment out of it to make it tolerable, but I was essentially in it for the money. I would not entirely recommend that priority.

Next, if you are going to partner with someone, be choosy as to who that someone is. Should it be a member of your family? I did that successfully, but in other cases there can be plenty of baggage that won't help. Carefully analyze your contemplated arrangement.

Then, grand-kiddies, save, save and save. This is so important. Note that there are a hundred perceived reasons why you can't do this. Maybe more. Start small. Establish a saving habit from your very first paycheck and keep at it religiously. You have a calculator, so use it. Try six percent. If you can't afford to save six percent of your paycheck, then figure out how to adjust your spending to allow yourself to do so.

If you have gotten comfortable with six percent, then try eight. Then try ten. Then twelve.

If you don't think that you need to do this, do some research. Access to the Internet is everywhere. Use it. See how the average American at 62 years old has done with saving. Fair warning: the American savings rate has been pathetic!

Another fair warning: it is likely that you may think, grand-kiddies, that there is plenty of time to start this discipline. This is not so. Every day that you delay is another day that you'll have to save on the other end of the whole process. There are plenty of poor Americans in their sixties who thought that there was plenty of time to start.

One other thing: learn about investing. No, it's not too early for this. Get some help. Read plenty. Most importantly, learn what compounding is. You will thank yourself later!

As I write these words, I have been retired for thirteen years. That would not have been possible had Jude and I not saved and invested. You can do this too, grandkids. Try to get started early! You will thank yourselves later.

And, yes, one other thing: pay attention to what is happening, sometimes in your own back yard. At times, opportunity is staring you right in the face, or perhaps, lurks just around the corner. Recognizing it may be a simple matter of being aware. Just proceed intelligently. Remember what the carpenters say: "Measure twice, cut once."

If you ever do get into business and it's not trending well, don't wait for it to suck you dry. If reasonable adjustments don't soon reverse the trend, cut your losses and move on. There is nothing shameful in that. Only inaction is shameful.

THESE PEOPLE HAVE GUNS... AND THEY USE THEM!

It was a big day for Sunshine. She brought her new boyfriend home to meet Jude and I for the first time. Turns out, Dave Fiore was the fellow she would marry, but we weren't sure of that at the time. However, the meeting did have the marks of a proverbial rite of passage.

Dave was certainly a likable enough fellow, not as "country" as we were, but that wasn't unusual. He was from a suburban area in Connecticut. He was obviously well educated. We all sat in our great room, draining a few beers and getting to know each other.

Sunshine's sister Vanessa and her husband, Drew, were there for the occasion. Cousin Krista Tucker had joined us, too. She adds zest to any gathering.

It should be here noted that Jude was ever-so-slightly on edge that day. Not on account of any social factors of the moment or that we were running low on beer, but rather because of the Berber. That's right, the brand-spanking new carpet on the great room floor.

My readers surely know the feeling. A new car, new furniture, new carpet—for a while, they are all painstakingly guarded against any spills, dropped crumbs or careless blemish. The day's guests, milling around with sundry hors d'oeuvres and jelly cakes, were sure to foul the new Berber at some point!

That aside, something altogether odd occurred. It was a bright and sunny day. I gazed through the big window to take in the outstanding scene. There, in broad daylight, a groundhog scooted across the lawn and took momentary refuge under a shrub, quite close to the house.

This set off alarms in my head. Sometimes when an animal's behavior is well out of the ordinary, as this was, it is a sign of rabies. It was most peculiar that the groundhog had found its way to the house, in the first place. If there was even a chance of rabies, the groundhog had to go. Groundhogs are bad news on a horse farm, anyway.

I politely excused myself and, with as much subtlety as I could muster, slipped outside and loaded my 12 gauge. It didn't take many passes in front of the house for me to spot the intruder. There he was, acting as though it was perfectly normal for him to be there. I attempted to position myself parallel to the house, so as to take a shot without firing into the foundation.

Unbeknownst to me, I had an audience inside the house. I had been carrying my shotgun over my shoulder. Krista was getting laughs, evoking notions of my likeness to Elmer Fudd. In the meantime, Sunshine's new beau couldn't believe it. Surely, I wasn't going to shoot the groundhog. As previously noted, he was from suburban Connecticut. I must simply be role-playing!

BOOM! The blast so startled our first-time guest that he hurled his beer four feet in the air before it splattered on the Berber. Score 1 for Dave Fiore! The groundhog was dead. Drew was happy that he hadn't been the first one to foul the Berber.

Apparently, when Dave got home, he was near effusive with stories about his in-laws to be. "These people have guns, and they use them," he told his friends.

Only when need be, Dave. Only when need be.

THE KIDS MARRIED WELL

Three for three. Who taught our kids to marry so well? After all, neither Jude nor I got it right the first time, but our kids did it right from the get-go. They got married and stayed married. Better yet, all of their spouses rank highly on the character scale. Jason, Sunshine and Vanessa all made good choices in the spouse department.

It's been very gratifying to watch the three families grow, to watch the same trials and tribulations of parenting that Jude and I went through, a generation later. If the job that our kids did is any indication, the instruction manuals have improved.

Sunshine's hubby, Dave Fiore, is a chemist. He was working for Beiersdorf Corp. (manufacturers of Nivea, Eucerin and others) in a quality control capacity. When Sunshine started pulling down some bucks, Dave bowed out from his job and went to work for the "Mister Mom" Corporation. His commute is much easier. He works in an altogether different quality control capacity than before.

Dave has done a remarkable job caring for the kids while Mom is busy bringing home the bacon. It may not be the typical course that most married couples follow, but who cares? It works for them. The only flaw that I can detect is that Dave is raising them to be UConn fans. This will hopefully not impair them too much through life.

Jason married the consummate mid-western lady. What a mom she has been, the kids having picked up her mannerly demeanor and striking good looks.

Becky's professional life has always been wrapped around writing, one way or another. Recently, she was hired by a company that needed a better social media presence, a better on-line posture. That company made a smart decision. This work is right in Becky's bailiwick.

Vanessa married Drew Haerle, a Jersey boy through and through. Drew earned his doctorate degree in the Rutgers Ceramic Engineering program. He is employed by Cabot MicroElectronics. His area of expertise is advanced semi-conductors.

Drew is always talking about a "slurry" that he is working on, used in the manufacture of the devices that his company makes. In fact, his most advanced slurry is in his margarita recipe, for which he is known far and wide. Beware when Drew starts talking slurries.

WOWED BY THE GRANDKIDS

Our three kids, Jason, Sunshine and Vanessa, all flew the coop for different states long ago. Therefore, Judy and I have been privy only to intermittent glimpses of our grandkids growing up. Whole point being, we can't take credit for the fact that they've grown to be such exemplary kids. Their parents get the kudos there.

Sports have been one of the highlights. Now age 18, Jackson is the oldest and has excelled in the not-so-common sport of water polo. Warning: This game is not for sissies! Those not in excellent physical condition need not apply.

At game time, two teams of six plus a goalie take to the pool. A goal net is at either end. For 4 periods of 13 minutes, players battle for possession of a ball that they propel into the net as many times as possible. All players are treading water for the full extent of time that they are in the game. (This old man gets tired just thinking about that.)

What goes on below the surface of the water is largely unseen, but a serious part of the game. Not as unseemly as the antics of ice hockey, but be assured that these guys are not being nice to each other. Bumps and bruises magically appear at the end of each game!

In 2016 Jackson was named to the First Team All Ohio for high school water polo. What an accomplishment! He scored 151 goals most recently, in his senior year.

Jackson's younger sister, Lauren, has become a swimming standout in her hometown of Mason, Ohio. As I write, she ranks 10th in the state in the 200 Individual Medley (IM). Her 200 Free Relay was 2nd in the state. Her 200 IM relay was 3rd in the state. Her Mason High School Girls Team finished 2nd in the state. Wow! Lauren is a sophomore.

In the meantime, how about our grandson Tucker Haerle? His high school is in Sutton, Massachusetts, where he is a junior. Two years ago, as a freshman, Tucker was the starting quarterback on his high school's varsity football team.

Despite the fact that Tuck has a gun for an arm, his coach has generally opted away from the passing game. During Tuck's most recent season, that didn't really matter. Tuck rushed for 1081 yards, setting his school's record. He was named to the Central Massachusetts High School Allstar team.

Tuck's sister, Annika, has been a dance standout. Ballet, jazz, tap; her repertoire grows and improves constantly. She is a pleasure to watch perform. As I write, Annika is age 15, but even as a small child, she was always dancing. Dancing is part of her makeup, her wiring, her mindset. It's no wonder that she excels.

On our fireplace mantel is a photo of Annika dancing in the froth of the waves at North Carolina's Outer Banks. It is an utterly majestic shot. How anyone could have struck such a pose, given a footing of wet sand, is beyond me.

Grandson Owen Fiore, more distinctively known as O. Dubbs Fiore, is multi-talented; talents that range beyond athletics. For example, Dubbs knows when to hold 'em, knows when to fold 'em, knows when to run away. How many card sharks do you know who can run like a gazelle? But Dubbs only runs when he has to, far less often than not. Owen taught his Grandpa how to play poker not long ago. I am forever indebted.

Owen and his sister, Maria "Sweet Cheeks" Fiore, reside in Cheshire, Connecticut. Maria runs like a gazelle, as well. (Rhyme not intended.) Both kids are involved in the whole spectrum of sports. Owen's in soccer, baseball, cross country and basketball. Maria is out there doing soccer, softball and basketball. They are young yet. They'll both be more formidable once they get more meat on their bones. In the meantime, they are on the field each day with good attitudes.

Would it not be grand for me to ascribe at least some of my grandkids' athletic prowess to my part of the gene pool? That's not going to happen, though. I have no part in the gene pool. Oh, well. I'll leave that one well enough alone. In the meantime, what a great bunch of kids... and athletes!

HOMESTEAD

TUCKER LANE

The lane leading to Tuckaway Farm has meandered through the woods a lot longer than the 60-plus years that any Tucker has lived along it. For that matter, a lot longer than any soul has lived, period. The lane serves eight or so residents, but it's not a publicly maintained road. Those eight residents take care of that.

So what was it originally? A path? A logging trail? A beekeeper's trail? Anyone who ever knew the answer to that question has long since passed on. An old house sits near the lane, maybe a hundred and fifty years old, maybe closer to two hundred. The origin of the lane may be a simpler story than any of us think. Somebody needed a path to get to this rather remote site before any building could commence.

Regardless, the lane is a present-day treasure to Alexandrians; walkers, bicyclers, hikers, horseback riders, even the occasional car. Motorized dirt bikes, however, are anathema. The lane seems to have a universally therapeutic quality. For starters, to travel it requires the passerby to slow down. That less hasty pace takes the traveler through a panorama of trees, leaves and wildlife. In the autumn, Tucker Lane is nothing short of a kaleidoscope of color.

Life on the lane hasn't always been as easy-going as it might appear now. Any road requires maintenance and potholes don't fix themselves. Anything less than a well-drained dirt road always has potholes. Sorry! Cars not belonging to visitors or service people are frowned upon. You see, cars cause the potholes. Most folks don't realize that.

Snow doesn't plow itself, either. Wouldn't that be grand, though? At the time of this writing, we "lanies," as we call ourselves, have never been better equipped with our own snow plowing equipment. It wasn't always that way. We depended on neighbors who had plows. I'm glad those days are over. It's way better not being beholden to someone else.

I fear that the lanies of the future may not be as Spartan as is required for this unusual lane paradigm of ours to continue. At some point, some lanies will cave, demanding that the road be maintained by the township. I don't care to be around for that. Our autonomy defines part of the paradigm. Good luck getting the township to take it over, anyway.

A TALE OF LONG LANES

What is with the Tuckers and their lanes? Are long, gravel lanes in our DNA? One would almost think so. Over the years, there seems to have evolved a lane litmus test. That test seems to have applied to all Tuckaways, wherever we've hung our hats.

The DNA must have come from Capoolong. The lane at Capoolong established the essential parameters for future Tuckaway lanes. First and foremost, it was a dirt lane, or gravel, if necessary. Most gravel lanes start out as dirt lanes. Occasional shale is added over the years. That eventually turns into dirt as tires wear their proverbial potholes.

Then crushed stone or gravel is eventually added as lane dwellers strive toward further improvement. If that continues for a few decades, why then you just might have yourself a bona fide gravel lane. The point here is that lanes become part of country folks' identity, part of their evolution, depending on just how much gravel has been laid down.

The lane at the original Tuckaway was much the same as at Capoolong. It was long. It gradually gave out onto a public road. At that point, could the house be seen from the road? No. We valued our privacy much more than that. Our house at Tuckaway is about 6/10ths of a mile from the public road. That seems to be enough distance. Well, maybe.

Brother Dave and his ex, Marianne, bought a farm just down the road. They named the place Tuckaway Two. The house was on a long dirt lane with plenty of potholes. Could the house be seen from where the lane met Rte. 625? Not a chance.

Mom and Dad bought a retirement place in Bradford Co., PA. The sign at the end of their long, dirt lane read Tuckaway Bradford. Was the house visible from that point? No way. However, a good part of their 8-acre pond was visible from Ameigh Valley Road.

Jude and I had a farm outside of metropolitan Bell Buckle, TN, yes, with a long lane. Was the house visible from Rte. 82? The roof was, barely! The lane at Tuckaway South was paved, but that wasn't our doing. It was that way when we bought it.

Does the reader see a pattern here?

Here's one that will be a shocker to everybody. Sometimes when Jude and I are traveling, we seek out the most remote areas that we can find. One such place that we happened upon is known as Bluegrass, West Virginia. It is the most breathtakingly beautiful countryside that I've ever laid eyes upon. We gazed at a lane that wound up a hill to a house; a lane that had to be easily twice the length of Tucker Lane.

We had to pay them a visit, if for no other reason than to compare notes on what motivated these folks to make this trek on a regular basis. Turns out, a single woman lived there.

Yes, she was a little surprised by our visit, but she appreciated it nonetheless. She recognized that we were on the same page.

The views from her place were spectacular. Flocks of sheep could be heard bleating, far off in the distance. The surrounds were that of a storybook. Our conversation soon waxed a bit philosophical. We touched upon the undertaking required to reach home each day.

"Look around," she said. "How can you be here and not know that it's all good? I am reminded of that every day."

We shook hands after a wonderful visit and drove back down the lane. We, too, were reminded of why we "tolerate" our long lane. It is all good!

DIRT IS BEAUTIFUL

We didn't subscribe to Newsweek magazine. I have to guess then, that Jude or I read the article, "Dirt is Beautiful" in a doctor's waiting room somewhere. I hope that the doctor will forgive us for tearing the page out. This was in 1981, so I will assume that he/she has gotten over it.

It's so eloquently written and on such a germane topic relative to our neck of the woods. It was written 35 years ago. If you can find it in your library or online, do have a read.

The kids were growing accustomed to life on a dirt road. Vanessa, then age nine and having read the article, was enthusiastic to the extent that she wrote a reply to the author in Macon, Georgia. I just wish we had made a copy of Vanessa's letter to him. He was so taken with her letter that of all the responses he had received from the article's publishing, he replied to Vanessa's first. His reply follows:

January 11, 1982
643 Forest Lake Drive
Macon, Georgia 31210

Dear Vanessa,

I'm very glad you liked "Dirt Is Beautiful" and I'm so sorry I haven't written back before now. I've been very busy since the story was published, and I received more than 100 responses to the story, so I finally put all the letters I got aside and let them wait until after the new year, when I could have time to write back to the people who liked my story. But I kept yours on top because it was my favorite, and I wanted to let you know how much it meant to me.

I know what you mean when you tell people you live "in the middle of nowhere." I used to tell people when I was growing up that I lived "in the boondocks." I'm glad you realized how great it is to live on a dirt road. When I was 9, I was hoping my road would get paved. But soon I was glad it was a dirt road, and after I was grown up I tried to stop them from paving it.

I hope you'll enjoy growing up on your dirt road. After you've grown up and become a woman, it'll be one of your favorite memories, I'm sure.

Tell your mother I'm very flattered she framed my article. More than anything, writers like to be flattered.

It's also nice to see someone of your age who writes so well. So many children nowadays don't seem to have that skill.

I hope that you and your family have a very happy year in 1982.

Sincerely,

Bryant Steele

HILLBILLIES MOVE IN

Prior to moving to Bradford County, Mom and Dad sold our old house at Tuckaway to folks who already lived in the township. Jude and I didn't really know them, but apparently it was their moving day. Down the lane came a huge load of furniture and household goods of every sort... on a hay wagon! It was being pulled by a 1947 FarmAll M tractor.

Though it initially appeared as such, turns out they were not Jed Clampett and his kin; they were the Kellys. Beth Kelly, formerly Beth Muhs and several years younger than I, grew up on her folks' farm a few miles from Tuckaway. With much of their stuff having been stored at the old farm, the Kelly family's moving method made sense. Why bother to rent a moving truck? Nonetheless, their grand entrance was quite rustic.

The Kellys have been great neighbors since their moving day. Turns out, their hillbilly-like arrival was deceiving. They are sophisticated folks. We have collaborated on many a farming pursuit over the years. They put numerous additions on our old house, turning it into something far more palatial than the rudimentary home of my youth.

However, I can still somewhat truthfully say while driving by it each day, "that's the house I grew up in." Folks seem so impressed. I just smile.

HIGHLANDERS ON THE RUNWAY

Alexandria Township Mayor and contiguous farm owner, Harry Swift (RIP), called me one morning, maybe 15 years ago. He asked whether I had already fed my cows that morning. Oh, shucks, I groaned. Yes I had, but they never came to the feed trough. That had been most unusual. Maybe they were just feeling a little lazy and would be along shortly.

Harry explained that there were several Scotch Highland cattle up on the runway of the local airport, a property also contiguous to Tuckaway. For the record, cattle don't generally belong on airport runways. But how was it that Harry thought that they were mine? I was one of many who owned cattle in the township. However, I was the only one who owned Highlanders. Guilty as charged, then.

For those not in the know, Scotch Highland cattle are easily distinguishable from other breeds. They have great, curved horns and long hair that cascades down over their eyes, allowing them a sweetly heralding look. They are outfitted for cold, formidable weather.

A few hundred years ago, rugged souls from the Scottish Highlands took some of their native cattle and settled in the western reaches of the Aleutian Islands. At length, they found the climate there so forbidding that they pulled up stakes and returned home, leaving behind some of their cattle. Fast-forward a hundred years and again there was a move to settle the Aleutians. The new settlers found that end of the islands thick with Scotch Highland cattle.

But I digress. I was able to commandeer a few local cowboys, lassos attached to their saddles, to go round up my Highlanders. It was a piece of cake for these cowboys. In no time my cows were back in the pasture, no lassos needed, no mishaps on the runway.

This time, I even locked the gate. The cows bolted straight to the trough and wolfed down every speck of grain that I'd left for them earlier. At times, the lowly farmer wishes that his cattle could talk, yea, even reason. What did they possibly expect to accomplish this morning by standing on the runway? Did they even realize that they missed their flight?

TREE FOLLIES

A century-old maple tree once stood proudly in the lawn at Tuckaway. I endeavored one day to prune some dying branches from it. To that end I climbed a ladder positioned to deliver me to a solid branch from which I could do some chain sawing.

Of the myriad branches of that old maple, this was the lowest one. This is not to say that it was a comfortable distance from the ground. Although a fall from it wouldn't have hurt, the sudden stop promised to be a different matter.

I had hoisted a rope from the ground, up and over the intended "working branch." That rope was tied to the handle of my chain saw. I climbed the ladder, perched upon my branch, steadied myself over to my rope and pulled my chain saw up to the working elevation. Commonly working alone, I would often contrive such arrangements.

However, I made one small, but crucial, mistake. My chain saw swung like a pendulum on its way up and managed to slam against the ladder, which was free from my stabilizing weight. The ladder, knocked off the branch against which it had been leaning, fell to the ground.

Dilemma! There I was. No one home, no one even within yelling distance. There was no feasible way to climb down out of the tree. Jumping was not an option. Damnation! What was I going to do?

Well, as long as I was up there, why not complete the work that I had climbed up to do? Maybe someone would happen by and notice the marooned idiot in a tree with no way to get down. So, I completed my chore. It didn't really take very long. You must understand, however, that there are often long stretches of time on Tucker Lane before anything, much less anybody, passes by. So, there I was, stuck for the long haul.

From the lane, I was within sight, but who would happen to notice me amongst the leaves? I would have to really yell if someone ventured by. The average passer-by is, understandably, not looking for people standing in nearby trees.

I became contemplative. What a gorgeous spot this is. Very quiet. I could see, through the leaves, an ancient, horse-drawn plow that a farmer of yesteryear had abandoned here on the farm. What had happened, anyway? At some point, the horse was unhitched and the plow left rusting to the vestiges of time. Had the poor chap plowed his last furrow?

What must the year have been? 1906? Maybe 1878? I think it's quiet around here now, but there were no tractors working in these fields then. A dove's coo in the distance was occasionally interrupted by the clamor of a spring-tooth harrow contending with rocks. It was being pulled by a team of handsome Shires.

But then, they would have been pretty high-end farm stock. This wasn't that prosperous a farm. So, maybe it was a team of Belgians. One way or another, the farmer of yesteryear was working about as hard as his horses. There was no seat on this plow. He was getting bounced around by every whim of that field's surface, and surely it had little mercy.

Presently a car turned in the lane. The driver spotted me and came to a halt below my tree. I don't remember the reason why neighbor Alex Wolfson came calling that day. I can only believe that it was fate. Imagine that, Alex, divinely inspired!

Scurrilous chap that he is, he posed a perfectly lucid, sensible question.

"Pete, what are you doing sitting up there?"

I explained. With that, Alex hoisted the ladder back up to my branch. My safe descent was thus insured. Of course! That was the reason Alex came down the lane that day.

It seems that we never quite know the why, the how and the who. Is that even for us to know? Indeed, the maple itself met its own fate many years ago, blowing over in a storm. I'm glad that I wasn't still in it. Funny how things happen to work out.

DUMPSTER DAY

For obvious reasons this reporter keeps an ear cocked regularly for a story that somehow lends itself to the subject of horses. This story does not. Pardon me, but I just found the local color to be irresistible. Somehow everything gets back to horses, anyway.

Now then, most of us make a trip to the township dumpsters on some Saturday morning or another. Thus engaged recently, I ventured down the lane, truck loaded with junk that had been gathering about the farm for a while.

At times, these dumpster trips become a sort of social pilgrimage; one never quite knows who one might see along the way. I suppose it's a guy thing, you know? Men's Morning Out... at the dump. Is there no justice?

Seeking to relax and totally enjoy this rite of spring, I struck a match to a fine cigar and in so doing took my eye off the lane for a second. A second was all it took. There I was, stuck in the ditch; furiously spattering mud all over the truck each time I attempted to back up, then pull out. At length, I surrendered and opted for a John Deere and a tow chain. My truck looked as though it had just done some serious four-wheeling.

The morning was off to a fine start. First, the utter humiliation of having to call my wife to ask her to come steer while I pulled with the tractor. A few pointed comments were made. But, we got the truck unstuck, junk and all, so off to the dumpster I went.

At the first stop sign on Airport Road, up pulled my old kindergarten buddy, Jack Hahola. Jack was on the same chore. His truck, a clunker throwback to the 1970s, was so heaped with farm junk that he was lucky the stuff wasn't tumbling out onto the road.

Giddy with the humor of his situation, Jack jumped laughingly out of his truck just to tell me that he couldn't get the old theme song from *Sanford and Son* out of his head. Jack admitted, though, that the next time he did this he was just going to park his truck by the dumpster and tell the boys to throw the whole thing in, truck and all.

Not much further, now on Schoolhouse Road, the Aversa boys, Tom and Sal, braked in the middle of the road to have a chat. Oh, the looks on their faces! Almost as though they never had a muddy truck. But we shared a good laugh. Not wanting to cause a traffic jam, on to the dumpster I proceeded.

At the dumpster now, my neighbor, Dave Ennis, was pulling out just as I was pulling in. Funny how the essence of a situation can be best captured in a few words. Dave pulled alongside my truck, took a careful look, and in perfect deadpan, said, "Guess it sucks to be you this morning."

FISH STORIES... WITH FUR

A few weeks ago, early in the morning, my wife and I were rubbing the sleep from our eyes over the first cup of coffee. The phone rang unexpectedly, given the hour. Our neighbor, Susan Rochelle, knowing that we'd soon be venturing outside to feed the horses, wanted to avert any startling surprises. She had been outside already and in our field near the house had spotted a "pretty big bear."

We thanked her and, of course, looked outside but when does one ever get to see the bear? Not that we didn't believe her. After all, Susan is a very credible woman and, indeed, there had been a number of bearsighting stories floating around the neighborhood.

But the question is always begged: just how big was the bear? All we knew is what we were told, that it was a "pretty big bear." That description, of course, leaves itself open to interpretation. Later in the morning we spoke again to Susan and she confirmed her previous story. It was a "huge bear."

Well, I guess we were off to the races. A little later that morning we heard that someone else had seen the bear. That person's description wasn't too far off from the first. The bear spotted had been "gigantic."

A pattern was developing. The descriptions of the bear were becoming incrementally grander. By 7:30 PM the bear was bordering on a lyric from an old Jimmy Buffett tune: "Kind of a Kodiak-lookin' fellow, about nineteen feet tall."

The next morning, I went out to feed the horses and I have to admit, I was looking over my shoulder a bit more than usual. MaybeI really would get to see the bear. What would I do if I came face to face with it? Again, a Jimmy Buffet lyric came to mind. Why, I'd look that big old bear square in the eye and say, "Mr. Bear, I love every hair on your twenty-seven acre body!"

Maybe someday there will be an app for reporting recently spotted bears about the countryside. Then, finally, we'll start hearing about Black Bears, not Kodiaks. But, wait a minute. Who is to say the app won't have an exaggeration meter? Then we'll be right back to square one.

A FUNNY THING HAPPENED ON THE WAY TO THE MAILBOX

Horse racing enthusiasts will immediately recognize "The Call to the Post," the bugler's alert to riders that it's time to take position at the starting gate. This writer is an enthusiast to the point that when my cell phone rings, what's heard is that proverbial bugle call.

Sometimes when I've mistakenly pushed the wrong button and turned the ringer volume to high, you might think that you're standing at trackside right there at Saratoga.

Tuck that away for a minute and let's go back into time a bit... maybe 40 or 45 years. The more senior among us might remember, on their black and white TVs, a comedian and pantomime artist named Red Skelton. He was hysterically funny.

My mind works in quizzical ways so a recent incident with my cell phone reminded me of an old Red Skelton skit. Picture a farmer toiling in the soil. While he kneels over, his old transistor radio falls unnoticed out of his pocket, and there it stays while pumpkin plants grow up around it.

Months later, while harvesting the pumpkins, the farmer discovers that the slight jarring of a certain pumpkin causes it to play music! One can imagine Skelton's pantomime as he copes with his musical pumpkin. Prize slapstick.

Now fast forward to this past winter. While I was extracting mail from my mailbox, my cell phone (unbeknownst to me) slipped off my belt into a snow bank. Off I went, none the wiser. Presently I missed the phone and commenced a search for it, but couldn't find the thing. A day went by searching for it until my astute wife remembered that we had stopped at the mailbox before heading down the lane.

The plan was for me to go up to the mailbox and listen for a ring while she called from the house. But, wouldn't you know? The snowplow had gone by, leaving a substantial pile of snow along the roadside in front of the boxes.

I stood there at this desolate scene when, what to my wondering ears, there came a distant, but familiar sound. Deep under the snow bank there sounded a muffled but audible "Call to the Post"! I bristled like a three-year-old ready to spring out of the gate. Furious digging soon yielded my phone from this magical, musical snow bank and I was off to the races.

Still works, that cell phone! Next time I want to get rid of the damned thing, I better try a little harder.

POST HOLE DIGGER BLUES

You'll see a lot of nice post and board fencing at Tuckaway these days. No fencing fairy waved a wand and made all that happen. In fact, years ago I worked assiduously on building fence. It is seriously hard work, especially doing it all by hand.

First, each fencing segment of each new paddock being created had to be dead straight, so fastidious layout was step one. Each post hole was hand dug, three feet deep, eight feet apart. No cheating! Stability and strength of the fence depended on that rule.

Sometimes hardpan (a dense layer of dirt below the uppermost topsoil layer) in the ground prevented that depth. When that happened, the individual post was set in concrete, enabling consistency of strength in the line. Of course, that extra step slowed the whole process, but it made for a job well done. I resolved, however, to speed the job up. .. ... auger, a tractor-powered post hole digger.

As a kid, I'd had a little experience with one. Neighbor Paul Fritsche had an auger. Think of it as a giant, 12-inch wide drill bit that digs a hole down to the desired three feet in a matter of minutes. Problem was, it is one of the most dangerous pieces of equipment on the farm, on anybody's farm.

That auger bit was turned by a drive shaft splined to the tractor's power take-off. The shaft was totally exposed and spinning next to anyone who was on the ground near it. Watch out for loose clothing! If the universal joint of that shaft happened to grab your sleeve, things could get ugly fast. For the record, it was common to have another guy standing next to the machine, helping the tractor operator to position the auger.

News had spread far and wide of a chap up in Sussex County. No, he didn't get any clothing caught in his auger, but he did place his foot in the wrong spot. The auger bit grabbed the toe of his shoe. He was working alone, so there was no one on the tractor to disengage the drive shaft. The tractor didn't know it was supposed to stop. The poor guy's body was corkscrewed down into that hole like it was just a bundle of rags. Rest his bloodied soul.

I had a near miss with my own post hole digger. Paul Fritsche taught me a trick when I was young. The auger bit would reach a strata of tough rock and refused to dig any further without the downward pressure of additional weight. That was easy; just sit on top of the auger's gearbox. That put direct weight on the knives of the auger, and would often do the trick.

Enter the old loose clothing complication. The universal joint of the shaft grabbed the back of my shirt and wouldn't let go. It tore off my shirt, then my pants, then my underwear until it had absolutely stripped me naked! I was incredibly lucky not to be mangled by the indifferent machine. It dropped me to the ground as though I was little more than excess dirt. Thank the Lord I wasn't part of the pile.

I shut the tractor off and stumbled up to the house. Jude was working outside and saw me approaching in my

, still clutching a clump of tattered
.gh prepared for Show and Tell. I had
with the Almighty. I had been very, very

, day, I have in my dresser a little cardboard box.
For , .y, in that box are the tattered cloth bits from that
day. E. .y so often I look at them and am reminded that, when
working with machinery, we can't be too careful.

TUCKAWAY FARM - A GATED COMMUNITY

I've always looked a little askance, a bit wryly, at the notion of a gated community. Oh, I understand the whole premise behind one. Surely they have their place. How better to keep the rabble out?

Tuckaway Farm, I occasionally jest, is a gated community too. In fact, it has more gates than most true gated communities! The gates, however, are not there to keep the "unwanteds" out, but rather to keep the "wanteds" in. What we don't do for horses!

There are other notable differences between Tuckaway and other gated communities. There is no sentry at our gate requesting name, rank and serial number. Horses and riders enter and exit of their own volition, all hours of the day.

There is no Homeowners Association at Tuckaway. Or, perhaps it could be said that Jude and I are the HOA. There are no rules, no regulations. When potholes need filling in the lane, well, we just do it. Or we pay somebody to do it. Nobody dictates when it will be done.

I guess this is where I sound off a bit about gated communities. It seems to me to be another bureaucracy, another layer of government. A little mini-government calling every blessed shot within one's immediate surrounds. Don't we all need that, down to every last blade of mowed grass?

These strictures are even written into the deeds of gated communities. Thus, people buy into these mini-gulags right from the onset. Given this, one supposes that this is what many people want. That's quite all right, no problem. Do understand, though, that I'll take my own gated community... where the gates are only for the gaited!

FOR THE SAKE OF POSTERITY

There are farm implements of a bygone era, abandoned here at Tuckaway for who knows what reason? They are: a horse-drawn sickle bar mower with Cyrus McCormick's name emblazoned on the side; the steel fangs of a loose hay claw that hung on a trolley in the eaves of the cavernous haymow; a one-bottom, horse-drawn plow that was left unhooked in the middle of a field.

Why do I now display these relics here on the farm? Firstly, for the sake of posterity. I am hoping that someday they will serve others as they do me today. They are my legacy and my connection to the past. I occasionally observe them in their rusted state and am moved to ponder, to ruminate, to pay homage to those who plowed the fields of yesterday.

One wonders just what happened here? Why was the plow left abandoned to time, to slowly sink halfway into the sod? As the plowman unhooked, had he just heard his last dinner bell? Had he just plowed his last furrow? At dinner, did he learn that tomorrow he'd be going off to war? Who will ever know?

Studying these tools gains us understanding of how they operated. They were not the push-button grain combine. They were not the power-steered, turbo-charged tractor. They were the stuff of toil, the stuff of brutally hard work. The farmer was working nearly as hard as his horses.

I never had opportunity to observe the operation of that old hay claw, but it pleases me to imagine the giant raptor biting huge amounts of loose hay from a flatbed wagon. Certainly some wide-eyed farm boy with his three-tine fork stood atop the pile, balancing himself in the softness of loosely flung hay watching Dad, with harnessed team, and heeding his signal to hoist the next clench of the steely jaws to an awaiting loft.

These scenes would make a painting more wondrous than any harvest that we see today. The Tuckaway of yesteryear must have been a compelling vista.

WHATEVER WILL BECOME OF THE FARM?

In a farming community, one of the proudest moments comes when the farm has been in the family for a hundred years. It is a time-honored milestone. At least three generations have been stewards of the land, perhaps four or five.

Our farm will not reach that milestone. I am the second generation. Our "thirds" flew the coop for different states some time ago. None are of the farming persuasion, but that's OK.

Over the years, how many farms have we seen succumb to the developer's excavator? Too many! On our farm, that specter has already been addressed. Some time ago, we took advantage of New Jersey's farmland preservation program. Tuckaway Farm has been deed-restricted to agricultural use, in perpetuity.

The day will come when Jude and I can walk over the horizon with the certainty that the farm will remain a farm. It may be that only farmers take solace in that knowledge, but I doubt that. In a way, our land is for all, for all who enter peacefully. Indeed, we are blessed here in Hunterdon County. May it be enjoyed for untold generations to come.

Much of the credit goes to the voters here in the county. The preservation program has been re-funded time and again. In so doing, residents have assured themselves that a beautiful slice of Heaven will forever be farming country. I see it as a legacy that I've been able, in a small way, to help pass down.

Aside from shepherding Tuckaway through the preservation process, Jude and I purchased another local farm with intent to preserve it, then sell it. I worked feverishly to get the old Criterion Pony Farm, then spruce it up as best I could. Auction day came in Spring of 2005. We were so excited!

At sale time, I had what was, unbeknownst to me at the time, a wicked MS related episode. Vertigo! As the auctioneer's hammer slammed down, I sat slumped in the audience unable to hold my head up. I was deathly ill, but I heard the winning bid. Mark it sold.

Jude and I were able to preserve over 100 acres in the township. There are those who will forever deride us because these financial transactions were to our benefit. Ages hence, this won't matter. The preserved farmland will.

HORSE TALES

FIELD TRIP

Let's call it the way it is! Sometimes, reporting for the Alexandria Equestrian Association (AEA) Newsletter is rigorous; at times, a grind. For example, I was recently assigned to cover events of the Winter Equestrian Festival at Palm Beach International Equestrian Center in Wellington, Florida.

So what if it was 80 degrees with bright sunshine in the middle of February, with palm trees everywhere. So what if there were world-class horses in every direction? So what if splendid restaurants beckoned at every turn. Even margaritas! It was that grueling 2½ hour flight getting here that really leveled the playing field.

The first night featured the $150,000 World Cup Grand Prix jumping competition. Forty-one horses from sixteen countries vied to qualify in the "jump off" round. Six horses made the cut. Unfortunately, the horses of both Alexandria Township competitors, Peter Leone and Chris Woschenko, grounded the top rail, disqualifying them for any advance. Not all was lost, however. American Laura Kraut, up on Cedric, bested the field.

Let's ponder something for a moment. This was world-class competition. Every horse and every rider in the arena was highly accomplished, highly talented. Each horse was a wallet-buster, for sure. That said, how many townships in how many counties of how many states of how many nations had more than one competitor in the arena? That's right. One! Alexandria Township, Hunterdon County, New Jersey, USA.

In the meantime, how about Wellington, Florida? Wow! One might call it the Bloomingdale's of equine locations. Hard to believe this was just scrub land fifteen years ago; now it had become thousands of acres of beautiful horse farms.

And, oh, the homes, the houses. I was admiring the beautiful houses when I saw a horse's head sticking out of one. Wait a second; these weren't houses at all. They were horse barns! Hey, I'm just a sodbuster from Alexandria Township. Pardon me while I kick the manure from my boots.

My stay in the Sunshine State was short-lived. My editor booked me onto a plane the next morning for yet another grueling assignment. And you guys think this is all lollipops and roses? Guess again.

HORSE DECISIONS

Mom and Dad made a good parenting decision in the early days. They didn't have much money, so they gave my siblings a choice. (I was too young to remember.) We could get a TV or a horse. Not both.

Apparently, the decision was easily made and that was a good thing. Over the years, horses have had a profound influence on my life. I've spent a whole lot of time on horseback, as have my siblings.

We named our first horses Chocolate & Vanilla. As you might guess, one was white and one was brown. They were older, plodding, grade horses, but apparently a package deal was made on two horses, not one. In any case they were well behaved, which was good, because we more or less taught ourselves how to ride.

Other local boys had horses, of course. The Knight boys on Rick Road had Minxie. Stevie Townsend owned a Shetland named Shaggy. Together with them, brother Dan rode across the countryside whenever he had the chance. This included an early morning stampede through Camp Marudy as Wally Knight, a practiced bugler, blew Reveille! It was a country boy's version of the street gang.

HEIDI AND THE HOSPITAL

Hell hath no fury
like a woman scorned.
        -Wm. Congreve

Heidi was one pretty little filly. Born in a Tuckaway pasture nearly thirty years ago, she still grazes at her birthplace. From that very day, she was walking the gait that the Middle Tennessee settlers bred into these horses prior to the Civil War. Heidi rides like a Cadillac, a comfy Tennessee Walking Horse.

Watching a new foal is always spectacular. Their legs never get any longer than on the day that they're born, so "wobbly" is the word evoked. Miraculously, however, by the end of day one, that foal is running the pasture every bit as fast as its mama. This is one of the delights of horse breeding. The unknowing observer would never predict the progress a newborn foal makes in less than twenty-four hours.

It is sometimes a bit of a guessing game as to the coloration of the newbie. Initially, Heidi looked to be a sorrel, but after a few months she darkened a bit and became a classic bay with black mane and tail. A white stripe on her face and two white socks rounded out her markings. To this day, she is one sharp-looking equine.

Not far past age two, it came time to put a saddle on Heidi. I loved breaking and training horses, but Heidi was not without challenges. I was no expert, but eventually Heidi and I shared a civil discourse. Like all animals, horses are self-preservationists. They need assurance that their trainer is not going to do anything to them that will hurt. Gentle persuasion is the order of the day.

Some horses, when under saddle, are a little "mental" about walking through a stream. In her early years, Heidi had this tendency. The particular spot that she refused to cross one day was not exactly ominous; a trickle of a stream. Nonetheless, a good trail horse must cross streams, no 'ifs' about it. This was where Heidi and me butted heads. One of us was going to win.

Heidi kept refusing, backing away from this innocuous brook as though she was being asked to swim the Delaware. I repeatedly reined her around and made her face the spot again, a little more boot heel in her ribs with each repetition. She finally snapped. She let go with a tumultuous buck, hurling me Lord knows how many feet into the air. I landed smack into the streambed with the steel heel of one of her shoes digging into my leg.

It seemed as though Heidi had won. Surely you recall the old adage about getting right back up into the saddle. That wasn't going to happen. I was a bloodied mess! Judy spied me walking up the driveway, pronounced limp and all, with no horse. Indeed, on that day, Hell had no fury like Heidi.

So, does the trainer make the horse do what the horse doesn't want to do? Apparently my persuasion hadn't been gentle enough. Most times, the trainer teaches the horse a lesson. This time, the horse taught the trainer a lesson. It's all in a day's work.

Judy and I "discussed" my situation. I didn't need to go to the doctor; I just needed to clean my wound. You should know that I was no kid at the time of this incident. In fact, I was running a publishing business. The next day I'd be back at it.

Accommodating soul that I am, off we went to the E.R. Maybe they did a bit better job of cleaning me up than we would have done, but shortly we were back home. My leg throbbed a bit, but my night was restful. Two days transpired with but occasional aches.

Then things changed. Instead of going to work the next day, I went back to the E.R. Pardon the vernacular, but my leg had "blowed up like a wood tick"! The doctor calmly explained the specter of blood clots and that I would have to be admitted immediately with bed rest and intravenous blood thinners.

I calmly explained to the doctor that that was impossible. I had two deadlines tomorrow and I had to be there. (I wasn't just being a jackass here. We were a skeleton crew. Cross-training? Who with?)

The doctor, again calmly, explained to me that I had two choices. I could go about my business and risk death or I could start immediate treatment in the hospital! Did I already mention that, apparently, Heidi had won? I arranged for a delivery of files from Tucker Publishing, a stone's throw from the hospital, and set up shop bedside, I.V. and all. This may not have been any way to run a business, but it was all I could do.

I spent eight days in that miserable hospital! Without skipping many beats, we managed to get a few of our publications on the press. This was before the days of e-mail, cell phones, texting and the like, but somehow we made it. I didn't even have any blood clots trying to pass through my heart, not that that would have stopped me.

Heidi and me soon came to see eye to eye. She got over her water-crossing phobia and developed into a very reliable, sound saddle horse. We've had several adventures over the years. Some years ago I and a few neighbors and our horse trailers drove to Island Beach State Park in New Jersey, where we rode our horses along the sunny Atlantic shore. The big, wide ocean is intimidating to the unknowing horse, but Heidi splashed in the froth of the waves just like it was another stream at Tuckaway.

On another occasion, we rode the massive battlefield at Gettysburg. Heidi scooted up and over Little Round Top as though it was just another blip in the landscape. What a ride we had that day. Thoughts of not only dead soldiers but also dead horses, were a sobering part of the day. Heidi just kept motoring along. She made even less of a fuss about that than some little brook in the woods.

RIDING WITH THE ALEXISES—ALWAYS A TRIP

Horseback riding poses the occasional unpredictable situation. Anyone who denies that hasn't ridden enough. One of those "funny but not so funny" situations occurred recently while Jude and I were riding with John and Maxine Alexis.

The setting was superb, far at the back of the sprawling township-owned farm on Rt. 513. We had just paused to watch a Northern Harrier hawk swoop on its prey in the near field. An endangered species with a magnificent wingspan, this bird is a pure joy to see.

Now we were in the ravine by the rushing water, the woods checkered with sycamore trees... one of Alexandria's more beautiful spots. To think that most residents will never even see it. Ah, the advantages of horseback!

John, in the lead, reached up to pull a twig out of the way. Turns out the twig was attached to a whole tree looming over his horse. It's funny how some things literally hang in the balance. Tugging at the twig was enough to bring the tree down onto the horse's withers. John was in a precarious spot.

Now, mind you, this was no huge tree, luckily. Maybe three or four inches in diameter, it nevertheless called for an immediate reaction from the rider, who needed to summon some instant adrenaline, some capable muscle and deft reflexes! But, hark! The name is Alexis. There's a reason they held the first Olympics in Greece.

How often have you heard someone's description of a car accident? "It just happened so fast!" Well, John's encounter with the tree happened even faster than that. Even so, it was like viewing action suspended in time. His horse was still moving forward, but how was John going to avoid the tree? Well, have you ever heard of the Limbo?

While lying flat on his back on the horse's rump, John curled his hands under the tree, muscled it up over his head and thrust the timber away to crash behind the horse. The horse barely broke stride. John was slightly ruffled but remained in his saddle. The rest of us just stared, our collective mouths agape with amazement. Little did we know at the time that we had just witnessed the world's first performance of the newest Olympic event: Tree Curling on Horseback!

All judges gave John a 9.9. And the AEA board is pondering the erection of a granite statue of Alexis the Greek on the grounds at Alexandria Park.

PALEOLITHIC PARK

Warning: This story contains some graphic scenes that may not be appropriate for all readers. The faint of heart should perhaps move to the next tale.

And let me add one more thing. It regards my wife. She has a seemingly illogical phobia, one that I have tried in vain to understand for many years. She is deathly afraid of birds. Big ones, tiny ones—doesn't matter; she can't get near them. Feathers or flapping wings anywhere near her is a real issue. I don't know, perhaps it was some trauma in a former life.

* * *

Now then, please join us; myself, my wife, and Mike Nolan on a recent horseback ride. The day is perfect. The sun is bright, the breeze is blowing, the horses are fast and we're having a splendid time. We'd ridden along some field edges and picked up the Foxwood Trail where it empties to Woolf

Road. We stopped there to chat with some neighbors and then rode on toward Alexandria Park.

What a gorgeous spot, along the edge of the Bush farm where the horses descend down through the woods and have to walk the stream bed for a stretch before ascending the opposite side bank and onto the park property. That region is just one of the gems here in the township.

On through the park we rode to the start of a new "nature trail" brought to us by local scouts. Further into the woods past the current extent of the trail, it starts to get a little remote. One almost forgets where one is. No roads. No houses, hardly even a sound; perhaps just the faint trickle of a tiny creek or a buzzing cicada. Otherwise, it could be anywhere deep in the woods.

Then I detected something pungent in the air, but I wasn't sure what it was. We rode further, but then had to stop to determine our next direction. At that point we clearly identified the odor of decaying flesh. There ahead of us a ray of sunlight beamed down through the trees as if it were a stage light focused on an actor. The grizzled comb of a huge turkey buzzard stuck out of a hole in a rotting carcass. The bird's slimy comb glistened in the light—the stuff of an Alfred Hitchcock movie.

Turkey buzzards are singularly ugly and pre-historic looking. As we stared, disgusted, we noticed that there were two buzzards there. No, six. No, dozens—swarming in a huge circle, a veritable frenzy around a dead whatever-it-was.

The scene recalled an illustration from an old National Geographic magazine, depicting pre-historic Cro-Magnon man at wood's edge, club in hand, watching a flock of giant vultures as they pick and peck at some Paleolithic road kill. Fast forward a few tens of thousands of years and you have this same scene at the outer reaches of Alexandria Park.

But it gets worse. Surveying the situation, we realized that to continue we would have to ride right close to the carcass and further disturb these grotesque birds. Then it hit me: This is going to flip Jude right out! She thinks she's got a phobia now, just wait. Let's ride and not look back, I suggested. Mike led the way, Jude was next and I took the rear.

The carcass was that of a deer. Not just a deer, but a very large one, a buck with a serious rack. Did we stop to count how many points? No! The stench was far too foul for that. Not to mention we were interrupting the birds' dinner. Alfred Hitchcock would have had a field day.

So that was our little equine romp in the park. Indeed, it was good to be riding back home. We'd learned one thing, though. There's a reason they call it the "nature trail."

TRAIL CLEARING WITH A TWIST

On a recent Sunday morning six AEA men ventured out to clear some trails of debris and deadfall from the rigors of the past winter. It's safe to say that there was no lack of testosterone in these woods. The men all showed up with the requisite tools: chain saws, clippers, etc.

We had been working at a fever pitch for a while, getting a lot done, when John Alexis brandished a remarkable tool. It had a long handle with a machete-like blade at one end. John wielded it with a vengeance, felling any stand of brush that dared get in his way.

The tool seemed to belong to a different culture; not surprising, since John is known to have spent time in the jungles of Africa. But while using it, John's personality seemed to change. He became frenzied, his eyes rolling to the back of his head with that sullen cloudiness of a shark ready to hit prey. Then he ruthlessly butchered another sapling.

Frankly, we all became a little concerned. The woman who joins him in bed at night is near and dear in our hearts, also. Another fellow on the work crew looked at me with a pained expression. "I wonder if Maxine is aware of this issue?"

GENTLEMEN, BEWARE!

Take heed, men. Nail your boots to the barn floor, cinch 'em up and lock the door. There's a new breed of women in the neighborhood. They are often mounted on horseback; they are singularly attractive and quite conspicuous.

Should you encounter them on your ride, bear a few things in mind. The wind is always at their backs, they will always ride toward you from higher ground. You are immediately at a disadvantage. Cowboy, turn your horse and ride the other way. You've just had a close brush with The Desperate Horsewives of Alexandria!

Who are these women? This writer hesitates to identify them individually. Some are AEA members, some are not. They are most often seen on the road between Everittstown and Frenchtown; that stretch where every other sign seems to read "Preserved Farmland."

Perhaps as they gain in notoriety, as they undoubtedly will, I'll name names. But in the meantime, men, give them a wide berth. They are the Desperate Horsewives. Leave them well enough alone!

IF A TREE FALLS IN THE WOODS...

Take it from an old newspaper guy; it's always disconcerting when a reporter gets 'scooped' on a story by a competing publication. I thought when I retired that that wouldn't happen anymore.

But the other day when I called AEA's Suzanne Stidworthy regarding a horseback incident worth writing about, Suzanne informed me that she had just been called by the Horse News on the same subject. D'oh! How did that happen? Well, I reasoned, so what? I'll write about this better than they will anyway! Who cares if it prints later than they do?

When will we learn that when we're riding a horse, it's really a partnership? You, the rider, don't always know best. That horse may be aware of something that you are not; something that might even save your life. Ask Suzanne Stidworthy.

Suzanne was recently riding Luke, a neighbor's horse. Luke and Suzanne had just started up a trail there at TripleCreek Farm when Luke let his rider knowthat he wasn't taking another step forward on that trail. Luke tends to get a bit contentious now and then, but this time he was dead serious! He wouldn't go forward on that trail another inch.

After a few moments of indecision, Suzanne decided not to argue with her mount. Horse and rider turned and headed the other way.

Just as they did, Suzannecould hear the sound of straining woodfiber that, heretofore, she hadn't noticed. Then the thunderous crash of a hugetree exactly where she and her horse had just been standing. Seems this was a case where it was smart for the rider to listen to the horse.

Hundreds of years ago, the philosopher George Berkeley once posed a question regarding a tree falling in the woods. If no one was even there, did it actually make a noise? Of course it did, Mr. Berkeley. Humans aren't the only critters in the woods, you know.

At Tuckaway Bradford. From left: Sue, Dave, me, Dan, Mom & Dad, circa 1992.

Now and again, the Scottish in me blooms! Spring 2005 in the parlor.

The old hacienda has come a long way! Summer 2011.

Two inspired intellects, then me. From left, Yours Truly, Rutgers roommates John Majchrzak and Steve Yost... a relationship that has spanned decades. Tuckaway, October 1997.

Pete Tucker

Tuckaway South view from the back patio, April 2011.

Those Scotch Highlanders sure are equipped for rugged weather. Winter 1991 at Tuckaway.

Old sandbox buddies since age two! Alexander(Arlo) Mitchell at a concert where he was sawing the fiddle and playing it hot in Walkersville, Maryland. April 25, 2013.

One would surmise that the herd was out! On the lawn, Summer 1982.

Family Reunion, Jude's side, at Outer Banks, N.C. Nearly 100 attended.
Our immediate family paused and posed in the sand: Standing from left-
Annika, Tucker, Vanessa and Drew Haerle, Yours Truly & Judy, Jason,
Becky, Jackson and Lauren Thomas.
Seated in front- Maria, Dave, Sunshine and Owen Fiore. July 20, 2015

Jude and me just enjoying the day. Island Beach State Park, NJ Oct. 21, 2010.

POETRY

MT. SALEM SECRETS

Was driving by Mt. Salem church today,
Just like a thousand times before.
I braked, for a reason yet unknown to me.
Perhaps, a visit with the days of yore.

The gravestones were cold and stoic,
Leaving very little for me to know
Of what happened here in centuries past
In the Alexandria of years ago.

But by and by the place warmed up.
The names on these stones, I presently found,
Are the names of folks I know today,
Many names that are still around.

There is Hyde and Hornbaker,
There is Kitchen and Race.
Justice Myers and Maxwell,
Mechling and Frace.

No, not all the names are still here.
Some took secrets to the grave.
But cleared fields that surround Mt. Salem
Are a measure of what they gave.

But off in the lingering corner,
Gravestones one can barely see.
Gnarled in briars and thicket and thorn,
Could anyone here explain to me?

Who are these folks? Stones worn of all clue;
Are they Mt. Salem's bereft and forgotten?
Who are these folks, at rest in tattered weeds?
Are they Mt. Salem's misbegotten?

The smallest of all gravestones,
And more overgrown than most,
Would become my day's challenge;
To reach it, the day's only boast.

So with clippers and shears, I take to the task
And whack and cut as much as I can.
Finally the stone is cleared, revealing two words.
How do you do, RACHEL ANN?

If, from your tiny grave you could talk,
What story would you tell?
Was life too short, was there time for play
Before your tragedy befell?

What ever was it that happened?
What ever was your now distant fate?
Was there not the time when you graced this place,
Before time declared it to be too late?

Now as you rest among these folks,
Though obscured by meddling weeds,
It is an honor to have finally found you.

Has Providence met both our needs?

Mine is simply to have found you.
The reason for my visit now comes clear.
I've passed you by a thousand times,
But now I know that you are here.

And do please know, Rachel Ann,
That for as long in Mt. Salem as I live,
Knowledge of your being here
To caring neighbors I shall give.

A.T.C.

A.T.C. carved initials in this tree
In Nineteen Hundred and Eight.
I never knew the chap.
Found his carvings much too late.

But his initials have long served notice
To the occasional passer by
That an oasis here beckons
To he who would but occupy.

A.T.'s choice was a beech tree
On which to leave his mark.
He knifed in the perfect condition.
He carved the perfect bark.

Shrewd of him to know, as well
That years later would come to be
A kinship at this wooded spot
Between me and A.T.C.

And how might that have happened?
How could it possibly be?
It's rather simple in retrospect.
We had a common tree!

No need to know the date in time
When cloaked by this canopy.
I know the beauty here is ageless.
Surely, too, did A.T.C.

We chat here on occasion.
I have questions about his life.
Was the world a gentler place, A.T.,
When you here wielded your knife?

Perhaps not, I venture to guess.
Shortly, the world was at war.
Were trenches in your future, A.T.?
Were you there when cannons roared?

I hope you stayed right here on the farm,
Your trenches, naught but windrows.
An empty haymow and threatening rain.
With luck, your only foes.

And do tell me, if you would, A.T.
Of this farm, some years ago.
I know of your toil, you left your tools.
That much I plainly know.

I've tried to keep up the farm,
Paying homage to your many a feat.
And do know that our spot still calls,
Here where the three streams meet.

I need tell you, though
Before it slips my mind.
If a walker might happen by today,
Your initials he will not find.

Nature's wrath; a storm years back,
Felled the beech; a cruel reminder.
Compare our wishes to Nature's way,
Our wishes are oft the kinder.

You see, A.T., my secret to tell,
Years after your mark in this tree,
I borrowed another page in its bark.
For decades it read 'P.T.'

In this place where we once carved,
Smaller beeches do yet grow.
Will others happen by to favor this place?
Providence shall only know.

We were both once blessed, A.T. and me.
Alas, it remains to see
If a wandering youngster happens by again
And discovers our canopy.

PETE'S PERSPECTIVE

LIFE THROWS ME A CURVE BALL

Somewhere in my early thirties my legs went numb. What the heck was going on? I could practically take a hammer to my ankles and not feel it. This eventually subsided, so I carried on. It remained a mystery. Fine—no big deal.

Not long afterward, I developed an inflammation in my eyes that was, well, annoying. I saw double, as well. You know what they say about men and going to the doctor, so I just ignored it for a while. Hey, it worked with my numb legs.

Eventually, however, I had to be examined because the problem didn't go away. Our family doctor called the eye condition optic neuritis, but he referred me to an optometrist for a second opinion. The optometrist concurred and prescribed a treatment that, he said, might take a week to clear it up. Further, he prescribed an appointment for me to go get an MRI, explaining that my condition is occasionally a precursor of something more serious: Multiple Sclerosis. An MRI would tell the story on that.

It did. Sure enough, I had MS.

This turned out to be my first of many MRIs over the years to monitor the progression of my disease. When I first received the diagnosis, of course, it was not good news, but there was hope. There was no cure, still is not, but people live with this disease. Life merely becomes more difficult.

First there was the delicate duty of telling the kids. This was a touching moment. Jason and Vanessa received the news with relative calm. Sunshine was so upset that she fainted. But we all had a hug and I assured them that nothing was going to change. Indeed, that was the case.

Over the years I have many times answered questions about MS from concerned people. I explain that I am essentially a walking short circuit. Everyone's body, you see, contains billions of nerves that convey electrical impulses back and forth to the brain. Think of these nerves as little wires. Electrical engineers know that any device that is properly built has wires that are sheathed with insulation to prevent electrical short-circuiting.

Every nerve in the body is thusly insulated. That insulation is called myelin. MS is actually a deterioration of that myelin, so as the disease progresses, there is more and more short-circuiting happening in my body. This short-circuiting manifests itself in many ways. I could write a book, but I won't.

In truth, MS has made my life more difficult, but I've been fortunate. I was able to work to age 49, which was when I aspired to retire anyway. Now and again I am forced to use a wheelchair, but most of the time I can still walk with a cane. Fatigue is chronic and I'm often unstable on my feet. Gastrointestinal issues plague me, but trust me, you don't want to read about that.

Oftentimes, my wife has to button my shirt, given that my fine motor skills are shot. It is a good thing I can type— well, hunt and peck—because handwriting is out of the question. I can't be on my feet for long at all. I have occasional bouts with debilitating vertigo. Other than this, things are pretty good.

MS has been a good lesson: whatever life throws at you, deal with it. Adjust. Nobody said this was going to be a picnic. Besides, I know so many people who are much worse off than I am. People who are in pain with cancer, people with a sickness or disease that is so debilitating that their lives have been gravely altered. Compared to this, MS is a walk in the park.

BREAKING THE MOLD

To one extent or another, we are a product of our parenting, probably to a greater extent than we realize. Attitudes toward race are no doubt propagated by parents that went before us. Given this, it is refreshing when somebody breaks the mold.

I know that Mom was exposed to racial bigotry when she was young. Perhaps it wasn't overt. If there is such a thing as "bigotry light," it is probably safe to say that the "N-word" wasn't slung in her household with great venom, but it was heard. I know this because as a very little kid, I recall hearing it from Grandma Schanze.

To the credit of both Mom and Dad, I never heard the word from them. They had broken whatever mold they'd been exposed to. Thankfully, they saw their way clear; they mustered the intellectual might to ban racism from their thinking. In his Sunday school class, Dad had his kids read aloud Dr. King's speech about his dream.

I was lucky to have parents who broke this mold. If it doesn't seem like much of an accomplishment, think about how racism has been interwoven in American society. It obviously does not go away easily, but it was never a part of us. Praise the Lord!

SUNDAY SCHOOL

I will say this about Mom and Dad: they got a whole lot of things right and they taught us the difference between right and wrong—but couldn't Sunday be a day to give it all a rest? That's what Sundays were for, right?

I recall distinct bitterness over the fact that we worked every week, double duty on weekends, but had to be in Sunday School every weekend. Then Church! Was there such a thing as a break? Maybe a little down time? But no... the cows had to be milked twice a day whether it was Sunday or not.

Much of Sunday School was oblique to me, abstruse. The teachers were not teachers by profession. They were farmer's wives, a banker, a janitor at a nearby school. I wondered if that would have made a difference anyway. I didn't know Leviticus. Who was he anyway? Was it OK for me to question? Did they really expect me to believe that God made the world in six days? If He was that good, why did it take Him so long?

Wait a minute. I had to toe the line here. Mom taught Sunday School. She did so for thirty years. Dad was a Deacon and taught Sunday School, too. Any problems that I had with all of this had better be kept to myself. Sunday School was just part of the dictum. Suck it up!

I developed a degree of cynicism listening to my folks rail about other church members; how they bickered over internal goings-on, how somebody wasn't holding up their end of whatever. Was everybody praising God here or just participating in Presbyterian Peyton Place? All of this, to what avail? I just wanted a day off.

My wife, Jude, had her church bouts as a kid, too. Her parents tried to raise a good Catholic girl, but Catholic school was not a positive experience for her. The nuns seemed to have a penchant for beating the kids. Between Jude and me, religious training hadn't worked out well.

Unfortunately, this whole Sunday thing left its scar. I am not a non-believer, but I was soured on Sunday to the point where I couldn't ask my kids to do what I had abhorred when I was their age. Much to their credit, they have all managed to shepherd their kids back into the church-going fold.

How did that happen? The Lord works in mysterious ways!

< WHITES | BLACKS >

While a junior in high school, I attended an international conference of students my age. It took place in Williamsburg, Virginia. This resulted from my state student council involvement and, in retrospect, one of the best lessons that I ever got from high school.

At the time America was in the throes of its civil rights movement. I was a lily-white kid from lily-white Hunterdon County, New Jersey. I was aware that the Reverend King had told us all of his dream. I knew that the Reverend Abernathy and his followers had wallowed in the mud at Resurrection City. I knew of public restrooms with divisive signage for Whites and Blacks, but nothing brought it home like a little first-hand exposure.

Three kids were in each hotel room at this conference. My roommates were a kid from Afghanistan and a kid from Tupelo, Mississippi. Initially, we did the usual awkward greetings. There was the understandable broken English of the Afghan. The guy from Tupelo was very tall, very reserved and very black. After getting to know each other a bit, we decided to go get a bite to eat.

Together we left our room and headed down the street a few blocks to a restaurant that had been recommended. The Afghani and I lead the trio, conversing about anything and everything that would allow better understanding of each other. Right away, the whole purpose of this international congregation was manifesting itself.

At length, I observed that we weren't being joined by our friend from Tupelo. He was lagging behind a good ten feet. I stopped and turned to the fellow, beckoning him to join our conversation. With seeming reluctance, he inched up to us and the three of us continued our walk. Almost to our restaurant, I noticed that our Tupelo buddy still was not part of the conversation and had dropped back a step or two.

Again, I stopped and turned to him, expressing my concern that perhaps I had said something to offend him. He shook his head, seeming a little discomforted.

"You don't understand," he said to me. "We don't do things like this where I come from."

I was befuddled. "What do you mean?"

"Where I come from, a black man doesn't walk down the street in front of a white man."

Please understand the context here. There I was, a wet-behind-the-ears country boy. In my neck of the woods, the racial diversity needle registered .001. Yet, there I was, looking squarely at the racial divide that convulsed America.

I thought for a moment. I smiled and put my hand on his shoulder and replied, "Well, how about walking down the street beside a white guy?"

He smiled faintly. I could see pain in his eyes. He obviously wasn't comfortable talking about this with a white person. But the ice had been broken. He had no choice but to get used to this. After all, we were roommates. We got comfortable with each other quickly.

As far as I was concerned, the conference could have ended right there. Tupelo would not have changed in the few days that it took him to return, but I think about him now and then. By any chance, did he return home with a slightly brighter view than the one with which he'd left?

If so, the trip to Williamsburg would have been worth it.

LOCAL COLOR á la TENNESSEE

Those early horse-buying trips to Tennessee were adventures in the area's culture. Local radio stations spoke volumes. It was early to mid-seventies. Country music was still all about twang. Serious twang. Buck Owens and Porter Wagoner were household names. War protesters were walking on the fightin' side of Merle Haggard.

Dad and I caught the local news while driving through McMinnville, TN. Apparently, a few area tough guys had been jailed the night before on charges that authorities were still attempting to determine. It sounded as though these guys hadn't broken any laws; rather they had just rubbed a local cop the wrong way. Regardless, they had appeared before the local judge that morning.

I write from a position of disadvantage here. I can remember the exact words of the newscaster, but you will have to embellish with your own Southern accent. The broadcaster announced the following: "They appeared in court with hair down to their shoulders and their shirts cut off at the armpits."

When the judge asked them all where they lived, they said we live nowhere, we live in the streets, whereupon the judge charged them all with vagrancy.

Ah, yes: Justice, Tennessee style.

POLITICS—A BRIEF STINT WAS TOO LONG

My involvement with politics became an odd enough compulsion later in my life. I already knew that it would wear thin, but I ran for office anyway, even though my heart wasn't really in it. I was not terribly confident, but I thought maybe I could do some good, locally. I ran for the lowest office in the county, that of Township Committeeman.

Don't ever say that your vote doesn't count: I won by one vote. At the time, my opponent wasn't getting on too well with his wife. She voted for me. Talk about a landslide!

The term was for three years. The Township Committee is the governing body of the municipality, in this case Alexandria Township. Meetings were monthly. I don't believe that I ever missed one, but beyond that, I made no big contribution. In those years, there were no major issues on the table anyway.

From 1981 to '83, Alexandria was a sleepy town. That worked out fine for a 29-year-old, greenhorn committeeman. After I served my term I did not run for another one, having no desire to do so. I guess that was my last endeavor, political or otherwise, that ended in my usual truncated fashion.

THE BRICK TAVERN AT PERRYVILLE

Interstate 78 links Pennsylvania's Lehigh Valley to New York City, and is a well-traveled highway. I recall the road being built. The quagmire of easements and legalities preparatory to construction was monumental. Speaking of monumental, in 1967 (I think), work crews moved the brick tavern at Perryville about 400 feet to make way for the road.

Ponder that for a moment: picking up and moving a brick building. Most likely the mortar between the bricks had gotten a bit brittle since 1813 when it was built. For perspective, consider that at the very moment that the last shingle was being nailed down on the building's roof, a mounted courier delivered the news of Commodore Perry's naval victory at the Battle of Lake Erie in the War of 1812. Workers therefore joyously dubbed the building The Perryville Inn.

I can recall the slow-moving task of the tavern being jacked up. Where was I when it was moved? Well, I didn't get off the farm much, but I heard tell they rolled it on logs. Talk about nerve-wracking! But, they moved it the relatively short distance to its current spot at Exit 12 intact.

History is grand, isn't it? How else would I be able to offer any such perspective about my own backyard? Ya gotta write it down.

Progress on Rt. 78 inched past Perryville for a short distance, then stalled for years before finding its way into Pennsylvania. In a way, this was illustrative of the lives of men who worked on the road.

One of my good childhood buddies was named Fisher Strom. Fisher's Dad worked on Rt.78 construction. The Stroms rented the next farmhouse over from Tuckaway. Fisher and I played together endlessly in the woods and fields. Then one day, Fisher was gone. The I-78 work crew had moved on.

I tried to imagine what that must have been like for Fisher's family. We'd just gotten to be good buds, and now they were gone like a drifting smoke. Writing this, I was prompted to Google Fisher, but to no avail. Fisher, if you're still out there, maybe you will read this someday.

Wouldn't it be grand to re-convene? Be warned though, I can't play Cowboys and Indians the way I used to.

PAST SHADOWS

It was very early 1960s, a pleasant enough day. Mom and Dad were out hoeing in the garden. An unfamiliar car bumped down the lane. When something like this happened, it was almost an event in itself. Not many unrecognizable cars ever appeared in our lane.

The car moved quite slowly and came to an odd-angled stop in front of our house, as if to suggest that the driver was unsure of his whereabouts. In the garden, Mom and Dad were about a hundred feet away when a couple emerged from the car.

From the distance, they looked to be a relatively young, maybe middle-aged couple, smartly dressed. The immediate impression was that these were not country folks. They slowly ambled out into the garden toward Mom and Dad, who had stopped work to size up the new arrivals.

The lady of the couple moved awkwardly, as if contending with heels in the newly tilled soil. As they moved closer, my folks saw that that indeed was the case. Mom and Dad exchanged greetings with these proper-looking folks. The woman had an obviously French accent.

"Are you, perchance, Janet Schanze?" she inquired of my mother.

Something was up here, Mom immediately deduced. Her name had not been Janet Schanze since her marriage to my father 16 years ago.

"I was Janet Schanze, I'm now Jan Tucker," Mom replied.

"Wonderful then!" the French lady said. "My name is Evelyne Powers. "I'm not sure how better to say this other than—I am your sister!"

For a fleeting moment there was awkward silence. Who was this French lady here in Tuckaway's garden? But it was already obvious that she knew enough as to suggest credibility. It was time to lay down the hoes, head up to the house and have some iced tea with these folks.

It turns out that it was Phillip, Evelyne's husband, who had encouraged her to make this trip. They had already made a similar visit to Mom's sister, my Aunt Laje, up on Quakertown Hill. Phillip, to his credit, had insisted that his Parisian wife introduce herself to her 'other' sisters.

Alfred Keyes Schanze, my Grandpa as has already been noted, sailed to Europe during WWI. He had met his first wife there. Two daughters had come of that marriage. Evelyne was one of them. Beyond the war, Grandpa had not been successful at convincing his wife to move to America, especially with two young children. Ultimately, Grandpa decided to sail back home without his wife and daughters.

Interestingly, I recently chanced upon a 408-page manuscript, typewritten by Grandpa one hundred years ago, in 1917. The title is Our Navy in France. Grandpa's ability to write puts mine to shame. He was masterful. There is not even a single mistake in the typewriting of it.

It is a fascinating memoir of his experiences sailing the Atlantic and venturing to France during WWI. He was an incredibly disciplined patriot. As I write my own memoir here, I take an occasional break and poke my head back into Grandpa's book. What inspiration it provides while I write these words!

I shall never know if Grandpa ever told his second wife, my Grandma Schanze, about his first wife that he had left back in Paris. He surely did not tell his two younger daughters. They had just found out today. Ah, the tangled webs that are woven.

Evelyne and Phillip Powers have long since passed on. They are both buried in the Tucker section of The Union Cemetery, Bethlehem Presbyterian Church, right there with Mom and Dad, the Schanze's, the Zimmers and the Gillons, all family names that have heretofore been mentioned. Rest their souls, one and all.

Judy and I pay them a visit each Christmas, if not more frequently. It is wonderful to have them all there, parents, grandparents, great grandparents; even the extended members, Phillip and Evelyne.

Family genes are quite remarkable. Mom, born and raised at Capoolong, her half-sister, born and raised in Paris, had handwriting that was exactly alike! Indistinguishable between the two. Now just how did that happen?

GETTING DAD OFF THE FARM

It was well past retirement time for Mom and Dad. They had long since quit their day jobs. Mom had been an executive secretary at Mack Trucks in Allentown, PA. Dad had been a workman's compensation claims investigator for the State of NJ. Any hay still being made on the farm was done by a neighboring farmer. There was no need for them to work anymore.

If only it was that easy to get the farmer off the farm! Or, to get the farmer to stop farming. Talk about it being in the DNA. Dad grew acres of strawberries. He sold them to farm stands. He had his own selling spot at Johnny's Truck Stop. He had a "pick your own" operation right there on the farm. He planted in the spring. He bedded them in the fall. He was consumed by the strawberry business.

It became obvious to Mom that she had to get Dad off the farm. Otherwise, he'd eventually drop dead in the field. I could see it myself. At length, Mom talked him into moving. Most folks, having reached such a point in their lives, opt for warmer weather; maybe in Florida.

Well, that was blasphemy to Mom and Dad. Other farmers in the region, some not ready to pack it in just yet, had moved to an area in Pennsylvania that was Hunterdon County all over again, maybe 30 years retro. Mom and Dad went looking for a peaceful spot in Bradford County, PA. Wow, did they find it!

Thirty acres, some of them wooded, some open, with a humble ranch house overlooking an eight-acre lake teeming with bass and catfish. Absolutely idyllic. If Mom and Dad couldn't relax here, they never would. But would they just stop working?

They had fourteen years of blissful retirement in this place. Aptly, a sign hung at the end of their long lane read: Tuckaway Bradford. They had most of the maintenance work done by local folks, so to the extent that they were capable, they did, indeed, relax. Mom and Dad had done it right.

Jude and I, our kids, nieces and nephews, my siblings: we all had great gatherings up in Bradford. Mom called one morning with the sad news that Dad had passed away during the night. Jude and I made the somber four-hour drive to be with Mom. She was holding up like a trooper. Dad's body was transported back home for burial. It was the end of an era, the beginning of a new one.

TOUGH STUFF TO WATCH

Dad died on Veterans Day, 2000. He had suffered for years with Parkinson's Disease. Sad how it goes; a man has a robust, very physical life and is then reduced to a bundle of tremulous nerves. He had a very sharp mind to the bitter end, however.

Clare was a bit of a paradox, a simple man who toiled on the farm, planted and harvested, as you now know. Yet, in his next breath, he could quote Shakespeare to an almost superhuman extent. His knowledge of poetry went well beyond Shakespeare. Clare Tucker was a well-educated man.

Toward the end, when Dad was barely hanging on, he announced two simple, short-term goals. He sought to live to the millennium change. He witnessed that. He knew that our daughter, Sunshine, was soon to be married. He wanted to be at her wedding. Indeed, Grandpa Tuck was there. He died seven days after Sunshine's wedding, as noted, on Veteran's Day. That, in its own way, was poetic.

Mom died eleven years later after a long and very gradual struggle with Alzheimer's Disease. After watching what both of my parents went through, I'm not sure which one was tougher to watch. At least Dad retained his wits to the end.

Mom completely lost her mental faculties. I, her own son, was "some nice man" who frequently came to her house to arrange her medicines for the upcoming week. She had no idea who I was, but I am happy to have been able to help her up to her dying day.

Ponder for a moment what you have been given by your parents. My first answer is "everything." They gave me life, for starters. Dad, with a wry smile, would have said, "Yeah, but that was the easy part."

But it wasn't easy! They worked hard. They did their best. When I ponder what it is that I owe them, indeed "everything" seems to be the best answer.

And, Dad, if I may have your ear from the grave for a moment: Regarding your angst about having pushed us kids too hard, don't worry about it. It was all in a day's work. Granted, you would have done things differently, had you a second chance. Wouldn't we all?

ON PARENTING

I do wonder what my good readers must be thinking. I suppose that there are as many different approaches to parenting as there are parents. Who has the right approach? Who has the wrong one? Can it even be defined in terms of right and wrong? Surely all the magazines have that one figured out by now.

My upbringing "down on the farm" was, I realize, not ordinary. To some of you, that may be classic understatement, but it was what it was. In the words of an old Willie Nelson tune, "There's nothing I can do about it now." Our childhood experience, that of each and every one of us, is the hand we were dealt. What we do about it depends on our ability to reconstruct it, and apply that reconstruction, later in life. Did that make us, did it make me, a better parent?

Who's to say? In my case, it happened so fast that it seemed there wasn't enough time to think about it before I was riding the horse myself. I do know this. I consciously chose to eliminate some of the details that were part of my childhood.

But isn't it curious, this thing called retrospection? I've said to myself now and again, wouldn't it have been better if I had more carefully duplicated some of my experiences to share with my kids?

Then, I think again: Ah, maybe not! They grew up on the same farm that I did and they turned out to be great kids. Now, how did that happen without them having to milk cows?

ALAS! RETIREMENT

I love the way people banter about retirement! What is retirement, anyway? A state of mind? An elusive dream? The time in our lives when we finally quit our job and work no more? Or, is it when we stop doing what we've been doing so that we can do something else? If there is one thing that is elusive it would be the definition of "retirement."

Are most folks who say they're retired actually retired? Wouldn't that depend on what their definition of retirement is in the first place? Will some people ever be able to retire? Are there those who never want to?

I retired in January of 2003, and I can tell you what my definition is. My definition is to live life day by day while doing whatever the hell I want to! So far, it's been a blast. I would recommend it.

This is not to say that I have all the money that I'll ever need. Talk about elusive. However, I will always remember my Dad when he would say, "to what avail, piling dollars on top of dollars? There will always be those of greater and lesser wealth than yourself."

OK, a youngster might say, but I can't just keep working for a wage. That won't allow me to retire. Good for you, youngster, to have thought enough about things to have figured that out. I would advise you to do something that too few Americans do anymore: learn how to make something, how to produce something. If that something takes machines to accomplish, so much the better.

So much the better chance that your something is being done on a large scale that will soon outweigh any wage that somebody chooses to pay you. I chose the advertising/publishing business. I never owned the machine. I never owned the building. I never had to. But many times I stood watching that web press disgorge my product by the thousands of copies. Lo and behold, I was producing something on a large scale.

However, if there is one tidbit of advice that I would render to those thus contemplating, it would be simple: start saving. It's not important how much. What is important is that you start now!

Do it with discipline. Do it every week.

Do not be afraid to take a risk or two; a smart risk, a calculated risk, one that you have analyzed carefully. What is the reward to be gained versus the risk?

If you doubt, as you will, if you suffer, as you will, remember this quote from Dean Briggs. "Do your work. Not just your work and nothing more, but a little more for the lavishing's sake, that little more which is worth all the rest." For my grandchildren who may be reading, there will never be a substitute for hard work, for smart work.

The day will come when retirement rewards you as it has me. May you be blessed with a long and enjoyable one. You are the one who will make it happen.

AND IN CONCLUSION

This is new territory for me. How does one end his memoirs? As if to say, "That's all, folks! From here on, there's nothing left to say!"

I prefer to suggest that you read my sequel in ten years. Oh, it promises to be colorful, if the first 62 have been any indication. But we never know, do we? Let's face it: whatever tomorrow or the next day holds for us is not for us to know.

I do know this, however; as I get older, I find myself going to a lot more funerals. I used to go to parties this frequently. It gets me to thinking. If I'm going to write my sequel in ten years, I better hurry up.

Obviously, we are each dealt our own hand. Mine was growing up on the farm. Could I have been dealt a better hand? Maybe, but I don't think so. I've lived a robust life, first and foremost, because I grew up on a farm. I have scratched the surface here of my childhood experience. If only I could remember it all.

I know one thing for sure, already. I'll no sooner finish writing my memoirs and some other memory will surface. Maybe five or ten. With each one, I'll be asking myself how on Earth I forgot that one. Such is the nature of it all. When I add up all of my memories from the farm, the list gets long. Lord knows how long it would be if I could remember everything. Thus far, it's been a life richly lived.

Pete Tucker

TRIBUTE TO JUDY

Where do I even begin? The greater dilemma; do I dare to end? Words are at once vacuous tinker tools of an enfeebled writer trying to express the inconceivable.

Judy has been, and is, my all; my reason to rise in the morning, my reason to sleep at night. When the day dawns and Judy is there, life begins anew. She is the fresh air of the morning; she defines my purpose for the day.

Some will suggest not to be so hopelessly devoted. Life is ethereal, you know. The norm of today may not exist tomorrow. With Judy, that is a chance that I am most willing to take, every day with quiescent mind.

Surely the day will come when death departs us. I will not bewilder myself with the notion. Why should I, while spending the day with Judy. When I ponder what we have endeavored together, what we have achieved together, how am I not immersed with a dramatic sense of fulfillment?... a sense that I must attribute to her. Having been on the same page with her for three, going on four decades has been a blessing beyond description

We've ridden horseback at the ocean's froth, skied Austria's Alps and France's Méribel. And, yes, we've owned that house on a hilltop high! Our beautiful kids now have beautiful kids. Life with Judy has been immersed in splendid things. Pondering now, is it any wonder that I am washed over by the memories. This is life as it should be, life with you, Judy, the love of my life.

My health issues are no secret now. My life is a bit of a struggle. Challenges abound and you handle my maladies with such grace and loving care. I notice that you have been a tad more inquisitive about things on the farm. How is this or that done? What tool is best to use? Subtle preparations, I suppose, for my waning years.

It is good that you so inquire; conversations need to be had. Remember, Jude, ours is life as it should be, whatever befalls us. I take comfort in knowing that you'll be fine when

I'm not here, that you are your own woman, that you've made provisions. And, God willing, we'll both find my words here to be far premature. But, how sad to have never written the words that I should have.

Love has a wonderfully abiding quality. Once given and nurtured, it does not die. I find great solace in knowing that ours will not. Between us, I am most likely to be the first to step over the horizon, but you may proceed in life with the knowledge that my love for you will never die. It shall always live and I am thus comforted.

I am prompted to fathom the sum total of my life's good fortunes, the whole of my sweet luck. They all point to you! I am eternally grateful that you have been my lover, my partner, my pillar and, indeed, my forever best friend... a debt that I could never repay. Bless you, my sweet one.

Photo by David W. Steele

Pete Tucker is a life-long resident of Pittstown, New Jersey. Meaning no disrespect to anyone's feats of higher learning, he holds a Doctorate degree from Hard Knocks University in Pittstown where his career entailed a quizzical mixture of occupations and assiduous study. He retired at 49 years old after selling his co-owned Tucker Publishing Co. in Flemington, New Jersey. Tucker and his wife, Judy, own most of the original family farm where they watch the horses graze and the hay being baled. Somebody has to do it! Tucker attributes many of his life's rewards and accomplishments to early life on the farm. He can be contacted at: tuckawaypete53@gmail.com.